Citizen Ninja

Stand Up to Power

by Mary Baker

RONIN Publishing, Inc.

Berkeley, California

Citizen Ninja

Stand Up to Power

by Mary Baker

Citizen Ninja: Stand Up To Power

Copyright 2016 by Mary Baker
ISBN: 978-1-57951-220-0

RONIN Publishing, Inc.
PO Box 3436
Oakland CA 94609

All rights reserved. No part of this book may be reporduced or transmitted in any form or by any means, electronic or mechanical including photo-copying, recording, or by any information storage and retrieval system, without written permission from the author or the publisher except for the inclusion of brief quotations in a review.

Production:
    Editor: Mark Estren, PhD
    Book Design: Beverly A. Potter, PhD
    Cover Design: Beverly A. Potter, PhD

Distributed to the trade by **Publishers Group West**

Library of Congress Card Number: 2016936562

Dedication

To Emma and Wyatt, my children and inspiration. May you and your generation pick up the mantle of civic duty and exercise your citizen power to sustain self-government for generations to come.

"Knowledge will forever govern ignorance, and a people who mean to be their own Governors must arm themselves with the power knowledge gives."

~James Madison

Acknowledgements

There are many to thank for making this book a reality. To the Holy Spirit for filling me with fire and purpose, to my husband Charlie, for being a sounding board, an enthusiastic Citizen Ninja student, and whose encouragement and support kept me going every step of the way, to my dear friend and colleague, Darcy Brandon who believed in *How to Become a Citizen Ninja* and was by my side for countless hours as we travelled up and down the coast teaching citizens how to be more effective activists, and to Pat Reeve, an activist role model who inspired me to speak up in the public square and do more than just show up.

Endless thanks and praise to Arne Ratermanis for his fun illustrations, to San Diego Foundation who generously let me quote them, and to all those who contributed to the arduous job of editing—with special thanks to Judy Greer, whose teaching career in English helped provide clarity in the early editing stages, Mark Estren, for asking questions to help me organize the content, and to Bev Potter for her patience, and whose expertise in authoring and publishing books made this book possible.

And finally, to the hundreds of citizens I work and interface with whose dedication to self-government inspired me to share the art of effective and sustaining activism with others—especially Orlean Koehle, Barbara Decker, Christine Meinsen, Greg Decker, Dan Titus, Don Dix, and Laura Douglas.

Table of Contents

Preface

I was born in the United States but grew up in Europe—Belgium, France, and Switzerland—and for nine years I attended French-speaking schools. At age 13, when my family moved to New York, I struggled to assimilate. I didn't fit into American culture, and my peers showed no interest in knowing about the one I had grown up in. To fit in, I dumped my European persona and superficially embraced this new world, but in my heart I was a teenager with *no identity.*

It wasn't until I was 22, in 1986, when I attended a professional baseball game, that I became an American in my heart. Tom Seaver was pitching one of his last games for the Red Sox against the New York Mets; the team he propelled to the World Series in 1969. The New York Mets fans were ecstatic because they were going to see "Tom Terrific" pitch his 300th win—he was still their hero. For the first time since moving back to the U.S., I stood up with over 60,000 American baseball fans and sang the National Anthem. Tears rolled down my cheeks as the powerful lyrics overwhelmed me. In that moment, I became not just a fan of baseball but a fan of America! I felt the surge of patriotism that would drive my devotion to this exceptional and inspiring country.

Over the years I reintegrated the European culture I had left behind and came to discover this blending of cultures was part of the U.S. immigrant experience. Though I have always been an American citizen on paper, at first I wasn't an American patriot. Like other naturalized citizens, I made the choice to learn about the *United States Constitution,* the

Bill of Rights, and the *Declaration of Independence.* I mem-
orized the Pledge of Allegiance and the National Anthem. I
studied America's system of government and participated
in elections. Eventually, I realized I was a citizen who had a
role to play not just in my community but in the society of
politics.

I am still learning and understanding the covenant of liberty our Founding Fathers and Framers forged for us in the
nation's founding documents. The work I do as an activist,
author, and educator is now part of my civic contribution
to safeguarding the American dream of life, liberty and the
pursuit of happiness—for all citizens and future generations.

Introduction

Do you worry about being marginalized for expressing your opinion in public? Have you been bullied in a town hall meeting or witnessed unethical behavior by your elected public servants? Are you fed up with politics but don't know how to effect change? Do you wonder if civil discourse is even possible? Are you passionate about a cause but don't know how to communicate it effectively? Do you feel powerless? If you answered "YES!" to any of these questions, then you are poised to step out of your routine to learn how to speak up with confidence, activate your civic rights, stand up to influential government agencies to effect change in your community!

Citizen Ninja teaches powerful strategies and tactics to help navigate the unpredictable world of politics and government. It's a guide for budding citizen activists—of any age—who want to engage but don't know how to start, what to do, or how to think about political activism. *Citizen Ninja* will educate, motivate, and activate you! By the end of the book you will understand why it is important to be involved in the civic process, you will see yourself as a Citizen Ninja with civic powers who can effectively stand up to dominant entities—including individuals, and governmental and non-governmental agencies—and you will be prepared to use your new skills to engage confidently in civil political activism.

> A guide for budding activists—of any age—who want to engage but don't know how to start.

What is a Citizen Ninja?

So what is a Citizen Ninja? While I was setting up a new domain name, a young sales rep helping me asked me curiously: "What is Citizen Ninja? I don't know what it means but I want to be one!" I explained that a Citizen Ninja is a person who is jealous of his intrinsic sovereign, independent and self-determining rights and whose temperament burns for freedom, truth, and justice. Citizen Ninjas don't wait for others to speak or stand up in their place when something alarms them; they are prepared, discerning, self-reliant, and assertive. They step out of their comfort zone and nimbly challenge powerful entities that disenfranchise the public and reduce their citizen power.

Citizen Ninjas are the people who respond to community issues by actively engaging city hall to make a difference. They are the Softball League coaches who talk to city council to address financial and field mismanagement issues, or the parents who demand that the city perform criminal background checks on their children's summer camp leaders and instructors. They are the elderly property owners who organize neighbors to testify at the city council meeting that new weed abatement ordinances are cost prohibitive for seniors on a fixed income. They are the young adults who request a town hall meeting to discuss the increase in gang violence and use of psychotropic drugs in their neighborhoods and how the city plans to curb the trend and provide a safer community.

> Citizen Ninjas respond to community issues by actively engaging city hall to make a difference.

Citizen Ninjas pay attention to government business and actively direct elected public servants to create policies that benefit the interests of the whole community such as balanced budgets, justified spending, public safety, natural resources management, and quality of life. They are the

Citizen Ninjas are smarter, more cunning, and more strategically savvy. activists who demand government transparency. They are watchdogs who speak out if there is corruption or ethical wrongdoing such as misappropriation of funds, a conflict of interest that leads to personal financial gain, or back room deals with preferred developers and builders. Citizen Ninjas are passionate about many different topics and know that civic participation places them in a better position of influence when new regulations, mandates, and ordinances are being considered.

Citizen Ninjas are activists whose objective is to preserve the power of self-government: a representative republic that is of the people, by the people, and for the people. They preserve it by actively engaging in the public square instead of passively allowing government agencies to make decisions on their behalf. They have passion but know that strong feelings are not enough. To be effective, Citizen Ninjas avoid throwing word bombs like "fascist pig" or "baby killer" to communicate their passion. Instead they strive to build trust by choosing words that find common ground and work toward constructive solutions. To gain respect, Citizen Ninjas focus on real problems that are tangible and have a direct impact on the community rather than arguing conspiracies or ideologies. Even when they can prove a conspiracy to be true, they are stealthy in their approach by using carefully chosen semantics so as not to diminish their credibility. They avoid having the tin foil hat placed on their heads if at all possible! They use the Citizen Ninja way to keep the lines of communication open so that all groups can progress toward tolerance, understanding, and solutions.

Citizen Ninjas have to be smarter, more cunning, and more strategically savvy to defeat highly organized government agencies, and powerful corporations and their non-governmental organizations partners. Showing up at a city council meeting, a public workshop, a rally, or a town hall meeting to express dissatisfaction is an important first step but good intentions don't make an effective citizen activist.

I became a Citizen Ninja

I didn't start off as a Citizen Ninja. I was just a regular member of the public who gradually became concerned about the direction the city was taking on proposed land use and zoning plans. I was particularly concerned about their economic impacts on small business in the region. My husband owns a small business and we were surprised to discover that the city's only business representation was a large electrical distribution corporation. It definitely was not small business! We decided I should attend the upcoming public workshop; a meeting where the public would have an opportunity to listen to a presentation of the plans and provide the working group with feedback.

As soon as it was obvious to the meeting facilitator that I was challenging some of the proposed plans and was not in support of them, she became unpleasant. In a kindergarten teacher voice she made light of my concerns, demeaning them as trivial. When I persisted with my comments, she responded in a derogatory tone accusing me of being naïve with no understanding of the issues and judged me to be someone who didn't like change. Her attempts to discredit me were vexing. My efforts to get back on message and away from the attacks were met with more verbal assaults by other attendees who

Bullies in public meetings squelch efforts to stand up to power.

demonstrated they had a stake in the project being approved. Two women sitting nearby barked orders at me to shut up and sit down so the meeting could proceed. I was not alone in this treatment; other people who disagreed with the plans being presented were treated with the same disdain. I left shortly after the encounter because I was startled and feeling like our citizen rights to voice our opinions had been entirely squashed by bullies.

I went into that public workshop with the expectation that self-government—the indispensable partnership between the government and the public—was still a foundational structure. Yet it seemed to be missing at this meeting. Why would the city call for a public workshop to get feedback from the community and then shut down opposition to the plan? Why not just take everyone's comments—for or against—and log them objectively? Why judge the opponents?

Predetermined Outcomes

The facilitator's approach made me wonder if there was an agenda, a desired outcome. Who were the players? Why was this plan so important to the working group and the city that they felt they had to marginalize its opponents? Why were the nonprofits and the experts mainly in support of the plan?

Facilitators of public meetings often have an agenda to get public compliance.

Where was the small business spokesperson? *Where were the citizens?* Was this an isolated incident or is suppression of opposing views going on everywhere? I felt utterly powerless, naïve, unprepared, and disillusioned. I could see others felt the same way. Maybe you have felt silenced in public meetings. If so, you are a candidate to become a Citizen Ninja.

That shocking experience did not thwart my desire to be involved; it had the opposite effect. Following that I attended other public meetings to see if they were equally predetermined and unjust. I discovered, that while not as extreme, they definitely had more subtle variations on the same theme: pressure to be a team player, little opportunity to speak—let alone to discuss the pros and cons, misleading information was given, instead there were prepared talking points with manipulative language, plus far fewer citizens compared to non-governmental organizations and experts who are pressing the proposed plans. These meetings led to more questions. Where is the tolerance for divergent opinions? Why not present the plans directly? Why the obfuscation?

Since then, I have worked diligently in civic and political affairs to safeguard fair and ethical political practices, to insist on a strong deliberative process during public meetings, and to teach others the importance of civic engagement and civil political discourse.

Stand Up to Power

How to Become a Citizen Ninja is a workshop in which I teach civic-oriented citizens—who wish to participate in the business of government and the political process but have no experience—how to speak up to power effectively and how to neutralize bullies. I explain that having passion is not enough to counter the agendas of large governmental agencies and non-governmental organizations. Let me repeat that—*passion is not enough!*

I have a passion for local issues, like land use, property rights, and quality education. To exert influence and effect change, to stand up to entrenched power, expose corruption and unethical practices, and stop government dictates I have civic knowledge, direction, strategy, tactics, and a network. Otherwise I am rendered ineffective and paralyzed like I was at that public workshop. I knew I was onto something with real impact when other activists flocked to my workshops to learn the Citizen Ninja way.

1

Be a Citizen Ninja

Becoming a Citizen Ninja takes practice. When you dedicate time to this endeavor you will learn to confidently navigate the wild political storms ahead. As a budding citizen activist you should know right off the bat that Citizen Ninjas are not engaging in the public square to force an agenda or an outcome that benefits their self-interests. Such motivation is insincere and results in frustration and loss of will to persevere because people resent being forced or controlled.

Citizen Ninjas are motivated by justice and truth and the unwavering belief that we, the people, are sovereign beings who have natural rights—rights that cannot be taken away by any person or government. We have the right to think independently, to determine our own course, and to make choices—good as well as bad ones. If our rights are diminished, we cannot preserve a free and just society where we can publicly deliberate the issues without fear of imprisonment, exclusion, being fired, or being fined.

As a Citizen Ninja you will become skilled in making deliberate choices to engage as well as learning how to handle people who accost you. You will learn to distinguish the right time to engage and be equipped with a set of tactics and skills to give you confidence. Being in the driver's seat gives you the power to control the conversation. If you start veering off course, you can disengage. The Citizen Ninja way produces thoughtful responses not emotional reactions.

> The Citizen Ninja way is an inspiring, fresh approach to grassroots activism.

The Citizen Ninja Way

- Become an expert! Knowledge is a powerful tool.
- Wake up! Recognize the bully tactics being used against you.
- Brush it off! Any attempt to manipulate you will backfire.
- Build coalitions! Network and forge alliances. There is strength in numbers.
- Be creative! Find different ways to communicate your message.
- Be patient! Successful activism is a process and takes time.
- Find courage! Distinguish real fear from perceived fear.
- Challenge! Choose your targets and challenge on your terms.
- Stick to your message! Expose fallacies and stick to your more powerful argument.
- Stay focused! Don't get sidetracked.
- Think strategically! Discern the environment and engage appropriately.
- Work locally! Focus on local public servants and hold them accountable.

Citizen Ninja aims to inspire the growing numbers of citizen activists from across the political spectrum. It is filled with examples that illustrate techniques and tactics. A single viewpoint is not advocated, rather there is a balance of examples derived from both liberal and conservative perspectives. Our nation has become so divided among political parties that

it might be tempting to believe an author must be advocating a single viewpoint when presenting examples that have political themes. In *Citizen Ninja* the views behind the issues are irrelevant, instead my examples illustrate Citizen Ninja techniques and are not meant to press a particular polical orientation. *Citizen Ninja* teaches how to make your voice heard effectively, whatever your personal beliefs may be.

Finally, you may be wondering how I came up with the term "Citizen Ninja", which conjures up the image of a formidable stealth agent shrouded in black from head to toe. Indeed, ninjas were highly trained mercenary warriors in medieval Japan. Samurai, which meant "one who serves' were indentured—property of the nobility—and expected to do as told. Samurai are famous for following bushido—the way of the warrior, which is loosely analogous to the concept of chivalry. By contrast, ninjas were Samurai who went rogue, acting covertly, cloaked and unseen, to break certain rules for an important purpose.

Citizen Ninja is a metaphor for activists who employ powerful non-traditional techniques to reclaim the power of self-government in the world of politics. The Citizen Ninja way is an inspiring, fresh approach to grassroots activism. Looking to the ninja warrior for inspiration in covert or indirect action, I used rallies, letters to the editor, and canvassing while imagining I was a political ninja—a powerful unseen force of change or a covert sentinel protecting the realm. *Citizen Ninja* shares a system of activist engagement that is discerning, flexible, confident, passionate, and exciting.

Citizen Ninja activists come in all shapes and sizes, are from all walks of life, and embrace a duty and a desire to impact local and national political struggles. The capacity to stand up to power is reminiscent of the Minutemen of 1775. While not engaged in an actual military battle,

Citizen Ninjas are engaged in a kind of cultural and ideological battle striving to restructure how government interacts with the public. While sorely lacking in resources and training, the revolutionary warriors were the Citizen Ninja activists who broke the rules of traditional warfare to triumph over the world's most powerful military. Now *that* is standing up to power!

The British Army had the might to squash the Colonial forces, so to stand up to such power the Minutemen, like the ninja of medieval Japan, broke the rules to their advantage. They invented guerrilla warfare—espionage, ambushes, and hand-to-hand combat. As with the Japanese ninja, be inspired by Minutemen fighters who defeated the highly organized, confident, and well-funded seat of entrenched power! The Citizen Ninja way uses the weapons of ideas, robust debate, respect, and tolerance to stand up to power, rather than the all-too-typical tactics of bullying and prejudice to cow opposition.

2
Speak Up

Aprovocative poem emerged a few decades ago that addresses the importance of activism and standing up to power. The words were inspired by impromptu speeches given by a German Protestant pastor during World War II. In this poem "they" refers to the Nazis.

> *First they came for the Communists, and I didn't speak out because I wasn't a Communist. Then they came for the trade unionists, and I didn't speak out because I wasn't a trade unionist. Then they came for the Jews, and I didn't speak out because I wasn't a Jew. Then they came for me and there was no one left to speak out for me.*
>
> —Pastor Martin Niemöller

Initially, Pastor Niemöller, a German nationalist, supported the early rise of the Nazi Party. He did not openly criticize Adolf Hitler and Nazism until later when the dictator pronounced that all churches were to submit to the supreme Reich Church of Germany. Niemöller's assertive condemnations eventually landed him in jail, followed by detainment in several concentration camps. He was released in 1945 by the Allied troops. Let's drill down into this.

When the Nazis started putting Communists in the camps, Niemöller disregarded the policy, saying: "Am I my brother's keeper?" When the Nazis later took the sick he confessed: "Perhaps it's right, these incurably sick people just cost the state money. They are just a burden to themselves and to others. Isn't it best for all concerned if they are taken out of the middle [of society]?" Only later, when he was in the camps, did Niemöller acknowledge personal responsibility for freely allowing the Nazis to exterminate the Jews and stated: "Mea culpa, mea culpa! We can talk ourselves out of it with the excuse that it would have cost me my head if I had spoken out."

Citizen Ninja trust but verify.

The last line of the poem reveals what happens if we sit on the sidelines in indifference, apathy, and fear. In an extreme event, there would not be anyone left to speak up. As Citizen Ninjas we understand that it is our responsibility to get involved sooner rather than later to uphold the republic for the sake of truth and justice. I share this story because I've heard people say: "Why should I be concerned? That situation has nothing to do with me! I don't need to get involved." This is an alarming attitude to have. If there is injustice or corruption by our government should we not speak up? Ultimately, isn't it in our best interest to get involved? The following examples highlight what two journalists, a political insider, a legal clerk, and a group of judicial activists did to expose corruption. Regardless of their titles or jobs, they are all American citizens who acted to uncover wrongdoing.

The only thing necessary for evil to triumph is for good men to do nothing.

EDMUND BURKE
18th c. Irish Statesman

Watergate, a political scandal that brought down President Richard Nixon, was exposed by two reporters from the *Washington Post* and a mysterious informant known as Deep Throat. Erin Brockovich is the legal clerk who was instrumental in exposing the alleged contamination of drinking water with hexavalent chromium by the Pacific Gas and Electric Company. The non-profit organization, Judicial Watch, filed seven Freedom of Information Act lawsuits against the US State Department demanding the release of documents having to do with Hillary Clinton's emails, and records about the Benghazi and Clinton Foundation investigations.

The Oath of Office

Elected public servants take an oath of office to publically promise and affirm they will defend the Constitution against all enemies both foreign *and* domestic.

I do solemnly swear (or affirm) that I will support and defend the Constitution of the United States against all enemies, foreign and domestic; that I will bear true faith and allegiance to the same; that I take this obligation freely, without any mental reservation or purpose of evasion; and that I will well and faithfully discharge the duties of the office on which I am about to enter: So help me God.

—Congressional Oath of Office

The Constitution sets the rules of law and prescribes the parameters of how government should operate. The Constitution is a document that protects our rights from an abusive and tyrannical government. All public servants take an oath of office including government officials, sheriffs, judges, and government employees. All swear allegiance to "support and defend the *Constitution of the United States.*" When public servants make this vow, Citizen Ninjas trust they are being sincere in their promise. They give public servants the benefit of the doubt. However, to verify and ensure they are staying on course, Citizen Ninjas continue to stay plugged in after elections. This communicates we are paying attention and we care. If we discover unethical practices, lack of transparency, corruption, or a dismissal of the people's wishes for example, we cry "Foul!" and demand proper recourse.

Becoming an Activist

Being an activist doesn't come naturally. It is a set of skills. Some people are soft spoken and sensitive and shy away from confrontation. It can take a while to feel confident to persevere even when feeling beaten. Instead of role modeling other citizen activists whose strategies and tactics may be stale, predictable, and unproductive, you are invited to follow the Citizen Ninja way. Typical activist go-to strategies are protests/rallies and informational meetings. These protests or rallies seem to cover the same topics and are held so frequently their members get bored and stop showing up, leading to low impact. Other activist organizations hold informational meetings with relevant speakers to educate the public about certain political topics in order to motivate their members to action. Great idea except there's no training offered to the public on how to engage nor are there specific calls to action. When we invest time as Citizen Ninjas we want to be fruitful and stimulating to make a difference even if at a localized level, which is where we can have an impact.

I began engaging in the political process by observing how City Council and County Board of Supervisors meetings proceeded. After attending a few, I noticed the majority of the people participating in the public comments portion of the agenda were not individuals, but rather organizations and businesses with an interest in the project being approved or defeated. I was surprised that the public was not there. There wasn't a balance of opinion being represented. Not understanding the importance of the public comment, I sought out my district County Supervisor to convey my concerns in private and to share my impressions and frustrations about the apparent lack of representation in the chambers.

I will always remember her response, which stunned me. Looking sternly at me, she carefully removed her reading glasses, laid them on the table and asked: "Where are *you* during these meetings? Why weren't *you* providing public comment?" Instead of the "Aha!" moment I'd imagined, I was having a "Duh!" moment. Her direct and pithy point corrected my approach to activism. It hadn't occurred to me it was important for *me* to inject *my* voice into the public comments.

Every two years, many of us campaign for candidates we support. Our activity ranges from discussing our views with friends and family, to donating money, walking precincts, and voting. Then after the election most go back to living their lives; working, playing, and raising families—failing to understand the importance of continued participation in government.

Start Small

Being a Citizen Ninja does not require being active on a full time basis; though many do! You can start by becoming aware of what is going on in your local government agencies—city council, school board, county board of supervisors, and metropolitan planning organizations. Look for opportunities for civic participation, which can be as small a step as discussing your views with your neighbor over the back fence.

Clvic participation includes reading the city council agenda online, attending meetings when there's an item on the agenda you care about, and speaking during public comment. How can our public servants accurately represent us without our participation? Lack of citizen involvement in the political process has led many elected public servants to believe they are elected to office to serve the special interests that got them elected—not the will of the people.

Elected public servants hire staff with various expertise to advise them and to do government work. Such staffers have considerable decision making power. They are the experts after all. However, having expertise does not mean the proposed budget, project, or plan is what is good for the city for whom they work. Elected public servants set strategic goals and the policies that direct the staff, which is why citizens need to speak up to their elected public servants. We must hold them accountable to their oath of office by agreeing or not with their agenda at Public Comment.

We're the boss, they're the employees who require supervision and guidance. Elected public servants do better with our support and attention. When we are part of the process, we are part of the solution.

Evolution of the Citizen Ninja Way

The Citizen Ninja way didn't develop overnight! In fact, I wasn't yet aware that by being a public speaker, pushing myself to meet one-on-one with public servants, attending workshops, conventions, and seminars, giving public comments, and volunteering for leadership positions in political organizations, I was developing powerful methods for civic engagement that would empower others.

Candidly, the tactics I am sharing in *Citizen Ninja* were motivated by self-preservation—I don't like being bullied, efficiency—I don't have a lot of time, impact—I don't want to waste time, and—comfort—I desire to improve my political environment. Through trial and error, I homed techniques to open channels of communication with family, friends, colleagues, public servants, and strangers. I persisted when unsuccessful, telling myself: "Well, that didn't work or that didn't feel good. I'll try another way!" When a tactic did work, I repeated it until, through practice, I became skilled, which gave me confidence to improvise. We—you and I—have precious little time in our lives to make an impact so let's be efficient and purposeful in our activism.

As I became engaged, other activists noticed that my approach was meeting with success and wanted to know my secret. How could I seem so relaxed when speaking to elected public servants—and they were listening! They wondered why I wasn't being heckled, dismissed, or marginalized. I explained that, because I know my *facts,* am *aware,* have *conviction,* come *equipped* with resources, tools, and tactics, and *prepare,* I feel confident and am able to *speak* with impact.

SPEAK UP WITH FACE

The Citizen Ninja way encourages a strategic approach to municipal engagement and civil political discourse instead of haphazard, emotional, spur of the moment outbursts. Preparing to speak up to face the public successfully with impact requires you to plan ahead and think about the best approach. FACE is the primer.

FACE

F—*Facts*

A—*Awareness*

C—*Conviction*

E—*Equip*

FACE helps us remember to know **F-facts**, to be **A-aware** of the environment, to have **C-conviction**, to be **E-equipped** with resources, tools, and tactics. With FACE you can feel confident when speaking because you are prepared. Let's look at each part of FACE.

Facts

To face the public successfully you first need facts. Citizen Ninjas resist emotional political arguments or ones based on personal ideology unless that's the point of the argument; to debate ideology. When we are out speaking in the public square—with the neighbor or at a Thanksgiving dinner with relatives—you absolutely need to know your facts if you want to avoid fiery entanglements.

Awareness

Being aware of your surroundings allows you to assess opportunities and decide how to engage. You want to feel good about what you are doing and to feel safe. Engaging the public in a passionate and professional manner can be challenging and intimidating if you are unaware of your environment. Citizen Nin-

jas are sharp-sighted and perceptive. When you leave your home to engage in the public square, put your head on a swivel to assess each situation so you can respond thoughtfully instead of emotionally.

Conviction

To act, you must have conviction. There has to be something that motivates you. Ask yourself what your hot button issues are. Ask yourself which news items drive you crazy when reported in the newspaper or on TV news programs. Are there trends in our culture that bother you? Have you experienced an injustice or witnessed corruption? As a Citizen Ninja, you know who you are and what you enjoy doing. Pick issues that prompt you to action and then channel your passion into effective activism by following the Citizen Ninja way. Activism should not feel like a chore though it can be hard work. Others will notice your passion and your success, and will want to work with you.

IMMIGRATION ◐
GLOBAL WARMING ◐
RACISM ◐
PRO-LIFE ◐
WAR ◐

Equip

Citizen Ninjas are equipped with tools and tactics. As a Citizen Ninja you know how to classify the person/s you are speaking with so you can have effective communication, you are dexterous dealing with bullies who want to shut you down, and you manage your resources so you have facts right at your fingertips. With an arsenal of options on how to engage you feel confident and brave.

TOOLS   TACTICS

Prepare

When not prepared, you will likely be anxious and fumble, coming
across as disorganized. You may
lose your train of thought or forget
what you intended to say. Other times,
thoughts may flood with too much information making it difficult to produce a coher-
ent argument. Mental preparation and
practice takes discipline and will power.

Prepare public comments ahead of
time; choosing each word carefully for
maximum impact. Research your topic so when confronted
with an opportunity to chat about it, you are prepared to
speak with ease. Being prepared empowers you.

Speak

Citizen Ninjas speak! This is crucial. Citizens who refrain
from participating in the municipal and political process miss
opportunities to share their ideas, opinions, or concerns
with their elected public servants. Their silence becomes a
tacit agreement to everything that is decided in city council,
school board, or county chambers. As a Citi-
zen Ninja, you understand the power you
wield when you engage in political discourse and speak.

Citizen Ninja teaches how to
engage strategically instead of
impulsively, and how to respond
rather than react to provocative situations. Your successes will empower you
to declare yourself as a Citizen Ninja—a
municipal warrior ready to do your part
to preserve a strong and healthy government of the people, by the people
and for the people.

3

Citizen Ninja Powers

Y ou need to develop Citizen Ninja powers before engaging the public. Without powers, citizens are weak, powerless, emotional, and likely to give up because they feel like victims rather than an empowered individual who can stand up to power.

My victim mentality was perceptible after being bullied at that public workshop. At first my anger was directed toward the bully facilitator with the kindergarten voice and her cohorts. Later it dissipated into a frustration with the system. "Can you believe they treated me that way? It was so rude. The meeting was totally fixed. They didn't allow for any disagreement! I wasn't the only one they bullied..." I told my husband and colleagues. Impugning the demeaning perpetrators felt good. But my tirades were useless and a waste of time; nothing was going to change until I altered my perspective and employed a more strategic approach.

Citizen Ninja Powers

✳ Civic Knowledge

✳ Self-Restraint

✳ Self-Assertion

✳ Self-Reliance

✵ Power of Civic Knowledge

Civic Knowledge is knowing the pertinent rules and laws, and understanding your civic rights within that framework. This allows you to safely yet boldly navigate the public square. Knowing the rules gives you the authority to expose people who are corrupt as well as agencies that bypass the robust consensus process.

✵ Power of Self-Restraint

Self-Restraint is discerning environments, situations, people, and issues *before* engaging. Purposefully identifying who you are talking to, the intensity of a situation, or the veracity of an issue allows you to have measured and strategic responses rather than emotional gut reactions. Citizen Ninjas are effective communicators when we are informed, yielding, calm and reasonable instead of angry and spouting desperate rants.

✵ Power of Self-Assertion

Self-Assertion is the willingness to step out of your comfort zone to engage in the public square. As a Citizen Ninja, you do this confidently because you practice and apply the Citizen Ninja way. The more you succeed, the more confidence grows as fears and ambivalence recede. When you declare your position, you seize opportunities to effect change and impact your community.

✵ Power of Self-Reliance

Self-Reliance is relying on yourself rather than waiting for someone else to lead. Citizen Ninjas are individuals who purposefully participate in civic affairs, engage in civil political discourse, and work with others in the community. This independence puts you in a powerful position because you are putting your trust and faith into your own action versus depending on others to speak or act on your behalf.

Leave the victim persona in the dust! The Citizen Ninja powers are the essence of Citizen Ninja activism. Exercising the four powers refines mental acuity and creates clarity of purpose. Like the ninja, who were elite tactical warriors, the powers are a mix of organization, skills, perception, and tactics that enable you to undertake tasks and missions with an exceptional level of integrity, precision, and poise.

Leave the victim persona in the dust!

4

Civic Knowledge

C ivic Knowledge is knowing about pertinent rules and laws, and understanding our civic rights within that framework. Simply knowing our rights is not enough, however. As Citizen Ninjas, we understand our responsibilities as citizens to make sure the laws are being followed and to act when the government infringes upon our rights. This is where the power of civic knowledge is greatest. Citizen Ninjas who use this power have the confidence that when they walk into a government agency meeting or workshop, or meet with an elected public servant, they can challenge anyone's illegal or unethical actions based on laws rather than on hunches.

Citizen Ninja Tyronne had a hunch that his local school district was unfairly awarding procurement contracts to a trustee's brother-in-law. Instead of making an unfounded claim at the next school board meeting, he requested public records to determine whether or not the trustee had broken the law. After reading through emails, requests for proposals, and reviewing the budget, it was clear there was cause for further investigation. He made this declaration at the school board meeting and the local district attorney took over from there.

Citizen Ninja Are Wise

As Citizen Ninjas we are not only familiar with pertinent laws, we understand their nuances and intentions. There are laws in every state of the union that legislate how public meetings are conducted and that uphold the importance of public transparency. Without civic knowledge, citizens would have no way of judging whether or not public servants were obfuscating the truth from the public. Let's look at examples of what happens when the public at large engages in the public square without the power of civic knowledge.

Elan was upset with a car dealership behind his house that was installing parking lights that shone into his bedroom. He complained to his neighbor, the contractor, and his attorney all without result. Elan didn't know that a complaint to the City Council would have been more effective.

Or consider Raquel who didn't know that it is illegal for elected public servants to accept gifts over a certain dollar value, so when friends told her they had gifted season football tickets to the mayor, not only did she not report it, she didn't connect the conflict of interest when her friends were awarded the city's alarm contract six months later.

Knowledge is Power

Just as parliamentarians who sit on boards observe *Robert's Rules of Order* on best practices of how to run a board meeting, Citizen Ninjas attend meetings to observe and comment on civic procedure. They analyze the government body with questions like: Does the public have access to records, agendas, public comments? Is

> Citizen Ninja are familiar with pertinent laws and understand their nuances and intentions.

all communication between staff and elected public servants transparent? Are all closed sessions legal? Is there an open bidding process for public projects? Are elected public servants disqualifying themselves when a conflict of interest presents itself? Most citizen do not even know which questions to ask if they were not familiar with the laws that exist to guide government agencies on proper conduct.

Citizen Ninja Rita found out that city staff was putting together an Ad Hoc Committee to address mobility issues on one of the main commercial/industrial corridors. Instead of being daunted by a large city hall, she contacted each City Council member, the City Manager, and the City Planner to set up individual appointments. At the meetings Rita explained that her background as a property/land appraiser would be useful and shared her interest in being selected to serve on the committee. Rita's civic knowledge served her well because she understood that transparency laws promote public participation even in the preliminary stages of a plan. Instead of waiting for the proposed plan to be presented to the public at large, she made personal connections with the decision makers and was ultimately selected to be part of the scoping plan.

Without civic knowledge people can't advocate for themselves, they don't know if laws have been broken, and they can't develop strategies to help them analyze situations, environments, or people. How can citizens participate in government and politics if they don't know the rules?

The power of civic knowledge helps identify opportunities for engagement. It also enlightens us and removes the veil of back-room dealings, nefarious conspiracies, and unethical behavior. Citizen Ninjas armed with the power of civic knowledge can stop corruption in its tracks!

5

Self-Restraint

Self-Restraint is discerning environments, situations, people, and issues before engaging. Citizen Ninjas are disciplined and trained in the Citizen Ninja way not to react impulsively to provocation. Use of the power of self-restraint awards us with time to assess situations so we can determine the best course of action. The art of discernment in political situations is a discipline that separates ordinary citizens from Citizen Ninjas.

Citizen Ninja Raymond used his power of self-restraint while attending a public workshop organized by the regional metropolitan planning organization. After listening to several people speak, Raymond realized his was a minority opinion. He was opposed to new bike lane plans that would take away a car lane to create more equitable street use between cars, pedestrians, buses, and bikes. He knew there would be unintended consequences, like increased congestion and pollution. Detecting that most of the proponents in the room were bike riders, Raymond knew that standing up and opposing the plan outright would be a waste of time. He was outnumbered and didn't want the crowd to lash out at him. Instead of placing himself in a vulnerable position, Raymond presented a fact that supported his view without letting the crowd know his opinion of the plan. He said, "Regardless of whether we are for or against removing a car lane, we should consider the EPA recognizes that as traffic congestion increases, air pollution becomes more intense, which increases health hazards." Raymond's statement caught their attention and encouraged less-vocal citizens to discuss alternatives to removing a car lane. In the end, the discussion was more balanced and the arguments were less emotional.

By contrast, Peter, who did not know the Citizen Ninja way, also attended the meeting because he owns a landscape business and believes that increased congestion caused by lane reductions will hurt his productivity. During the comment period, Peter expressed his objections to the plan. "This plan is outrageous! It hurts small business and affects productivity. If bikers want to bike they can go somewhere else. Bikers never pay attention to traffic laws anyway and they hog the road. They are a traffic hazard to law abiding drivers!" Peter's emotional comments, lack of factual data, and personal attacks side-tracked productive discussion about the pros and cons of the plan. Bikers attacked Peter and less-vocal citizens who might have sympathized with his worries about potential loss of productivity stayed quiet.

Avoid Emotional Presentations

Too often, well-intentioned citizens rely on emotions and personal ideology when expressing disfavor. Speaking passionately is one thing but an unabashed emotional outburst is another. No one likes to be yelled at or humiliated, especially in public. When citizens are not disciplined and restrained, they are viewed as troublesome and extreme. Once they are labeled as conspiracy theorists, verbal bomb-throwers, or nuts, they lose their power to persuade. They are no longer seen as reasonable and credible people who can have rational, objective discussions.

Many people figuratively burn their bridges and create a point of no return as in Peter's case. Similarily there are many who remain mute even when they strongly disagree with an issue. Their silence or their choice not to be involved communicates apathy and indifference. Sometimes people are silent to restrain overwhelming emotions. They are frozen by their sensations of fear. Peter's jibes caused a chain reaction of bullying behavior by the bikers, which hurt Peter's credibility. Often people restrain themselves from disagreeing for fear of this sort of retaliation. Had Peter used self-restraint, the discussion would likely have focused on Peter's concerns for small business instead of his opinion of bikers. When we allow our emotions to cloud our judgment or provoke us into action without assessing the situation, we risk losing our power.

Credibility

Blurting out whatever we're thinking causes problem. Lack of self-restraint prevents us from having meaningful dialogue with people, and hurts our credibility.

During a planning board meeting, Denise rudely interrupted the proceedings by calling one of the members a liar and accused the entire board of conspiring with a local environmental group to close public hiking trails in the region.

Twenty minutes later when it was her turn to speak at the podium about the planning board's trail maintenance plans, no one listened to her. Even if her allegations were true, no one paid attention because she was rude and had no facts.

To succeed in civil discourse, Citizen Ninjas begin with self-restraint. Recognize emotions that provoke or bind you and channel them. Then transform the way you think about activism. Many people believe that activism gives them the license to be rude, to provoke, and to bully. But speaking in the public square or standing up to powerful entities is not about acting out in anger, condoning violence, or relying on mean-spirited tactics. It's about honesty, building trust, treating others with respect, working towards constructive solutions, and effective communication. The foundation for all of this is the power and the discipline of self-restraint.

6

Self-Assertion

S elf-Assertion is the willingness to step out of your comfort zone and engage in the public square. A government that is of the people, by the people, and for the people requires the Citizen Ninja power of self-assertion. Self-assertion is the act of engaging and declaring one's rights, and in the world of government it is evident when citizens are engaged in their community.

A citizenry that is not assertive is not working to sustain self-government and risks giving the impression that it agrees to be passive and is okay with yielding its decision-making power to elected and non-elected public servants and bureaucrats. To establish our commitment to self-government, we Citizen Ninjas need to engage in four ways: civic, electoral, political, and social.

Civic Engagement

Personal *civic* actions, like volunteering to clean up local trails or empty lots, interacting with youth programs, being on a senior volunteer squad, or sharing professional skills with less advantaged adults are ways to enhance the quality of life in a community.

For example, Citizen Ninja Makayla runs a beauty pageant with the support of a local Lions Club. Every year, a Miss and a Junior Miss and their court of princesses win the opportunity to spend a year with Makayla learning about civic service. They attend ribbon cuttings with the Mayor, visit senior homes, animal shelters, and the vet hospital, and volunteer for civic and charitable events. Makayla is teaching these young women civic knowledge and the importance of munic-ipal engagement by providing a platform for volunteering and fulfilling their role as goodwill ambassadors for the city.

Electoral Engagement

Electoral activity such as voting every two years is one of our fundamental rights as citizens. It's surprising how many registered voters don't show up at the polls to cast their vote AND how many citizens are not even registered to vote. This has to change. If you are not registered to vote and want to be a Citizen Ninja, the first thing you have to do is register. You can fill out voter registration cards online, at any local government agency like the post of-fice, Department of Motor Vehicles, your city/town hall or county registrar's office, or you can typically locate a voter registration booth at local street fairs.

The experience of actively becoming a registered voter gives us a sense of pride and a greater awareness of our civic responsibility to pay attention to politics and to ac-tively participate. It's a great feeling! Voting in every elec-tion clinches our sense of duty and shows our commitment to the process of freedom. Even though we may not agree on who the best candidate may be for a position, we are united in our actions as voters. This is powerful.

Political Engagement

Political engagement is where the rubber meets the road. It is through these activities that you really demonstrate your passion for self-government. Giving a public comment at a local school board meeting, organizing a rally in support of or in protest to an issue, or meeting with elected and non-elected public servants are all ways you can assert yourself in the political dimension. These types of actions effect change. For example, Citizen Ninja Trevor and his sister Vanessa approached their local school board to address the district's poor effort to highlight African American heroes during Black History month. They took the initiative and offered to help the district put together a more meaningful program for the future.

Social Engagement

An additional measure that sets Citizen Ninjas apart from other citizens: social engagement. Political discourse is not exclusive to the government sphere. As we may have already experienced or witnessed, there is plenty of unproductive and emotional political discourse that happens within the social dimension of our daily lives. As a result, political discourse in social situations has become taboo in civil society and most of us will avoid it if we can. Civil political discourse can occur and have positive outcomes if you are willing to adjust your approach.

For years, I was afraid to bring up controversial topics such as capital punishment, welfare, and right to life versus choice, because these politicized issues would cause extreme irritation and anger in friends and acquaintances who held different opinions from mine. It was frustrating because having civil discourse on topics like these is paramount to advancing our society. I didn't give up trying and little by little realized that if I took a more strategic approach, I could have those 'hot topic' conversations and emerge unruffled by using the power of self-assertion.

Speak With a Gentle Tongue

The Citizen Ninja power of self-assertion requires us to use our self-restraint first. When we are in a social environment and would like to engage in political discourse it behooves you not to blurt out your opinion, especially when there is disagreement and emotions are charged. That approach aggravates tempers or creates divisions because generally people feel an immediate need to defend their position. Using the power of self-restraint Citizen Ninjas first understand the person's opinion on the subject by asking a question and then try to find something to agree on. From there we can gently assert ourselves and mix in our thoughts on the subject—facts are even better. This adjustment can yield great conversations and deepen everyone's understanding of the conflicting issues.

Citizen Ninja Jeremiah and his wife Wendy are both conservative and were dining with Wendy's parents, who are both liberal. They were enjoying a nice evening when the discussion turned to the upcoming presidential election. Frustrated with the two-party system in the United States, Jeanne, Wendy's mother, stated: "Our country is experiencing a crisis in leadership. We have two corrupt political parties in a broken two-party system and everyone points fingers at each other. Ugh. And now the Republicans have ten candidates to three Democrats. How do we know which one to trust?"

Mike, Wendy's father, responded brusquely: "Another election, another Republican clown car!" Being a Citizen Ninja, Jeremiah didn't react to this indirect insult. Instead he asked his father-in-law to explain what he meant by the comment. "I don't agree with Jeanne," he declared. "I am more philosophically aligned with the Democrat party and I don't think the fact that there are two parties is fundamentally part of the problem. If conservative media were more balanced it would help."

Though Jeremiah does not agree with Mike on the issue of conservative media bias, he quickly seizes the opportunity to agree with Mike about the two-party system. "Philosophically, I too am more aligned with my party—the Republican party." Wendy interjects: "But I'm equally as frustrated as Mom is by the distinct lack of cooperation between the two parties and the finger-pointing." Jeremiah queries: "Couldn't this lack of cooperation and finger-pointing also be viewed as balance?" The evening ended on a pleasant note because Jeremiah found common ground with his father-in-law and asserted his views in a respectful and gentle manner. There is little doubt that had Jeremiah chosen to react angrily to Mike's clown-car insult, the conversation would never have reached deeper levels of discourse.

Have a Game Plan

Self-assertion in civic, electoral, political, and social measures fosters dialogue, and when combined with civic knowledge and self-restraint it promotes civil discourse and meaningful activity. The power of self-assertion can test your resolve when you are not meeting with some success.

Consider Melinda who was trying to motivate Historical Society members to attend city council meetings on a regular basis while the city was updating its general plan. Instead of providing logical reasons for why they should engage, such as impactful zoning changes, she criticized them for being lazy, apathetic, and ignorant. No one responded and eventually she gave up.

Just like Ninja warriors who study their targets so they can strike with pinpoint precision, we have objectives, strategies, tactics, and tools.

Objectives

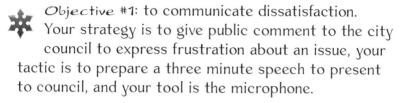

Objective #1: to communicate dissatisfaction. Your strategy is to give public comment to the city council to express frustration about an issue, your tactic is to prepare a three minute speech to present to council, and your tool is the microphone.

Objective #2: to disrupt a plan. Your strategy is to hold a rally to protest an initiative, your tactic is to advertise your event on social media, and your tool is signs.

Objective #3: to educate the uninformed about a candidate. Your strategy is to precinct walk to introduce him/her, your tactic is to create informative literature to inform citizens about the candidate, and your tool is the pamphlet.

To engage without a game plan is an unproductive use of time and energy, and furthermore has the potential for unfavorable results. Clear objectives, strategies, tactics, and tools are the Citizen Ninja techniques we are going to learn together to be effective and assertive in the public square.

7

Self-Reliance

C itizen Ninjas who rely on themselves to effect change wield the power of self-reliance. The United States was forged by active and committed individuals who relied on their courage, strengths and skills to rebel against dominant powers. The Colonial forces chose to sacrifice their lives (and sometimes their families) for the belief that personal freedom and the liberties of future generations were more important than the life being prescribed to them by a British monarchy.

Brave African Americans broke through the lines of entrenched segregation in the Southern States, generating a historic civil rights movement. There was no other organized body they could rely on to stand up to power, so they coalesced with like-minded individuals and made a personal choice to rebel against oppression. Citizen Ninjas use the power of self-reliance to step up to be watchdogs, to participate in government and community, to expose corruption, and to engage in political civil discourse. Self-reliance promotes a powerful self-government which in turn perpetuates freedom and justice for all.

Citizen Ninja watchdogs take personal responsibility for witnessing how elected public servants are governing on our behalf. We show up at local council, planning, and board meetings, read the agenda, and submit a public comment card when warranted. We participate in public workshops and town hall meetings so that our ideas and opinions are shared. When city council puts out a survey asking how the city should prioritize spending general funds, Citizen Ninjas take the time to fill it out. Our voice directs and influences our public servants' decision-making process before items are voted on. We don't rely on others to speak for us; we speak up instead.

For example, consider John and Ellynn, property owners in a small town, who don't know the Citizen Ninja way. They don't read the local newspaper, they've never been to a city council meeting, and they ignored a mailer from city hall announcing an upcoming council workshop to get community feedback on proposed plans to build a round-a-bout at the bottom of their street. They also missed the council meeting that cinched a unanimous vote to approve the project because the majority of people who participated endorsed the round-a-bout plan.

A year later, after a contractor had been approved for the project, the city sent a notice to homeowners in the area informing them there would be traffic delays during construction of the round-a-bout—taking John and Ellynn completely by surprise. They hated the idea of a round-a-bout and were upset that they weren't informed. They called the Mayor to complain but there was nothing the Mayor could do because the city had followed proper procedures to inform the public.

Citizen Ninjas Darla and Will, on the other hand, did show up at the council workshop to give their feedback. They, too, live near the proposed construction site and didn't like the idea of a round-a-bout because of unnecessary expenditures. The existing intersection was adequate, and besides, there weren't safe pedestrian crossings in the design. Their remarks started a series of questions by council to the staff members, which lead to the staff being directed to add safer crosswalks. When the final proposed plan was presented by staff to council, Darla and Will voiced their objections at the public mic. Though the council voted 5-0 to support it, Darla and Will were satisfied that at least by participating, safer crosswalks were incorporated into the design. Unlike John and Ellynn, who could only react to the situation, Darla and Will were proactive and provided a degree of influence.

Of course Citizen Ninjas who take personal responsibility to be civically engaged don't always get their way. In the case of Citizen Ninjas Darla and Will, their participation did not stop the round-a-bout, but their speaking up accomplished two things: they informed city council and the public that not everyone was in favor of the project, and their safe crosswalk concerns impacted the final product. You aren't always going to agree with the decisions made by elected public servants, nor will a community always agree with one another about the best course to take. However, you can expect that a governing board like a city council will foster proper participation and public deliberation so that competing positive values are considered and debated.

Start Locally

Self-reliance is easier at the local level because government offices are nearby. It doesn't take a lot of time to walk, drive, bike, or take public transportation to attend a school board meeting. Live video streaming and recording technology is usually available, so if homebound or traveling we can watch the meeting from a computer. Meetings at the County level are a little more challenging to get to because their meetings are frequent and are typically held during working hours. Fortunately, Citizen Ninjas who want to keep abreast of County government can also avail themselves of online video technology.

When government is remote, it is a challenge to keep informed. Despite our best efforts to be self-reliant, we might miss import-

ant events. Often we have to be personally impacted to realize there is something amiss. For example, the US Army Corps of Engineers and the US Forest Service were closing hiking trails in the Southwest region of New Mexico and making them off limits to the public, with no explanation. Because hikers, mountain bikers, and equestrian enthusiasts were personally affected, they engaged their County district representatives to get answers. Eventually, the County sheriff was directed to investigate. He made inquiries with both Federal agencies and demanded they follow the law and coordinate their activities locally. Finally portions of the trails were reopened, though some remained closed due to dangerous conditions. When a small band of self-reliant Citizen Ninjas took personal responsibility to find answers to their questions, the missteps taken by the two Federal agencies were exposed and the situation resolved.

Tackle Federal Issues Locally

The Common Core State Standards (CCSS) program is an example of how Citizen Ninjas can still have an impact locally even when government decisions are made far from the local level. CCSS are K-12 education standards written and copyrighted by a corporation, and not by a consortium of States, as the title suggests. The decision to market these standards was made by the US Department of Education secretary and their adoption as state standards was made by a majority of state-level education committees across the country. With very short notice, school districts, school board trustees, teachers, parents, students, and taxpayers were suddenly faced with accepting new standards and associated costs, without any robust public deliberation on their merits. Furthermore, private entities, like the corporation that wrote CCSS, are not subject to the same transparency laws that government agencies are. The public cannot file a Freedom of Information request for records, file for redress of grievances, or request changes in the standards to make them more suitable to the needs of a local district. How can self-reliant Citizen Ninjas who do not favor initiatives like CCSS stand up to powerful partnerships between governmental and non-governmental agencies and corporations?

Policies or initiatives that come from the federal level can be tackled locally, so the key is to broach issues like CCSS there. Citizen Ninjas, interface with school board trustees and request transparency, communication, and accountability in order to keep track of how the new standards are impacting the students' quality of education.

For example, Citizen Ninja Leti and her cohorts requested trustees form a Citizens' Budget Review Committee, a Technology Review Committee, and one for Curriculum Review to foster an open and transparent process for appointing citizen volunteers detailed proposed budgets, strategies for appropriate and safe technology use in the classrooms, and curriculum overview and goals for K-12. The school board trustees approved the three committees and appointed fifteen citizens to serve. By the end of the process, school board trustees received a report from staff and heard recommendations by the appointed volunteers. The synergy between the district staff and the public allowed for maximum transparency and helped the trustees make more informed decisions.

Citizen Ninja Sam started an "Opt-Out of Standardized Tests" campaign to let parents know that they had the right to opt their children out of the multiple CCSS assessments. As a retired teacher, Sam saw teachers being pressured by principals to teach to the test. He knew the number of assessments was interfering with classroom time. Sam invited friends with children in high school to attend a coffee at his house where he explained the campaign. Then he asked for three volunteers to host a coffee so he could inform their friends. After Sam spoke at five such info sessions, people started to take their own initiative to spread the word. As a result, an estimated 5% of the junior class opted-out. They planned to reach out to elementary school parents the following year.

Personal Initiative

In both cases, Leti and Marcus did not wait for someone else to stand up and take action. They each took a personal initiative to effect change. The power of self-reliance inspires us to participate in government and politics using our own initiative so that we can hold our elected public servants accountable to us. Remember that we are the boss and they are our employees. It is up to us to maintain self-government that is of the people, by the people, and for the people. In his book, *Restoring America: One County at a Time,* Joel McDurmon aptly states, "You have to make the choice for liberty. By leaving the decision for someone else, you have abdicated your responsibility."

Make the choice for liberty!

JOEL McDURMON
21st c. scholar

8

Govern For, Not Over Us

As Citizen Ninjas, we expect that our elected public servants to govern *for* us and not *over* us. We make the choice to participate in government, stand up to dominant power, and be political watchdogs because we support and want to protect a representative republic that is of the people, by the people, and for the people. We the people *consent* to be governed by individuals we elect. Our government is structured so that the greatest seat of power is at the local level—town, city, county. This keeps government close to the people and where Citizen Ninjas can be the most effective. Local government is where local issues are presented, debated, and solved by a relationship between elected individuals who make up City Councils, School Boards, and County Boards of Supervisors, and the people who are their constituents.

We Are the Power

Local government is so vital to a free society that the Tenth Amendment to the *Constitution of the United States* reserves for the States and their people *all* powers not delegated to the federal government. The Framers of the Constitution determined that the federal government should focus on specific, limited obliga-

tions, enumerated in Article 1, Section 8, that in summary include commerce regulation, national defense, and jurisprudence. For example, the federal government sets standards for weights and measures and regulates trade for interstate and foreign commerce, it declares war and maintains military forces to protect our borders, and it sets laws such as ones that protect copyrights and patents.

The Framers purposefully intended that the federal government have significantly less authority to govern the people at local levels. The federal government is not supposed to interfere with the States' powers to establish local government and public schools, to conduct elections, regulate trade within their borders, and provide for public safety and public works. Nor can it inject itself in local city, town, and county jurisdictions that have control over land use, fire and police services, zoning, and code enforcement, for example. If the federal government deems it necessary to impose itself, it must officially coordinate with local agencies. Fundamentally, our government is *just* when it protects individual and States' rights, and it is strong and healthy when the public participates. We are the true power! When Citizen Ninjas engage, we are exercising our civic powers to direct and influence the electorate.

Grassroots

Civil society in America is the glue that holds us together, and it is informed by the fundamental truths and rights enshrined in the *Declaration of Independence* and the *Constitution.* Civil society saturates our culture. It refers to individuals and organizations in a society that are independent of the government and include non-profit (NPO) and non-governmental (NGO) citizen organizations.

In America, we are entitled as individuals to function as members of society. American civil society supports the individual—within the paradigms of family, religious institutions, business, and the rule of law. These institutions of civil society have created prosperity, charity, and liberty. The civil rights and the suffragette movements are examples of what can be accomplished when civil society works together at the grassroots level. Citizen Ninjas are an integral part of civil society because they are the active members in our towns who respond to community issues and engage with city hall to make a difference. They are the people who are actively directing their elected public servants to create policies that benefit the interest of the whole community. They are the volunteers who make up service organizations like the Friends of the Public Library and the Senior Police Patrol, or initiate causes like the Clean and Green Squad, or start a local chapter of Safe Routes to Schools.

Governance by Stakeholders

Institutions of civil society bring like-minded people together to stand up for causes that would be difficult to undertake if they were acting alone. This is great as long as our system of government is based on equal representation of self-governing individuals. But this is not what I witnessed in that first public workshop or others that I attended thereafter. I went to the meetings expecting to observe an instrumental working relationship between the public and the city council working group; instead saw the voice of civil society groups (NPO/NGOs) drown out the singular voice of the citizens—ours.

Stakeholders are individuals or groups that have an interest in public policy.

Equally distressing was the disproportionate ratio of constituents to business and NPO/NGO associations who were there speaking on our behalf and helping the government agency to create policy. This is a shift in power from self-government to governance by *stakeholders*. Stakeholders are individuals or groups that have an interest in public policy. By wielding their civic powers, Citizen Ninjas reclaim their rightful place at the stakeholder table.

Citizen Ninja Jay found out the County Board of Supervisors was considering zoning changes near a local wetlands preserve to accommodate a new residential mixed-use facility. Without hesitation, he called his district representative to relay his concerns about the preserve and related potential environmental impacts. His district rep told him not to worry, that the staff under the Board's direction had pulled together a variety of economic and land use experts (stakeholders) to study impacts and opportunities, as well as work with the project developer, contractor, and architect.

When Jay asked to be a part of the committee as a citizen representative, the district rep dismissed him. "It's not necessary. Our staff will manage." After pressing his concerns with all five County Board Commissioners, Jay was finally invited to be part of the committee as a citizen stakeholder. Jay used all of his Citizen Ninja civic powers: he knew the rules, he was professional, he didn't take no for an answer, and he took the lead instead of waiting for someone else to address the situation.

Public Private Partnerships

As beginner Citizen Ninjas, it's important for you to be aware
of the imbalance of governance that is happening in our
society. Quietly, without fanfare, our cherished local government—individuals participating in civic decisions—is being
replaced by regional governance, which is a further step
from us and less representative. Federal and State agencies
are facilitating partnerships between public and private entities. This is not necessarily an undesirable alliance. But when
non-elected government agencies, boards and commissions,
favored businesses, and an elite civil society are the primary
stakeholder partners, proper representation suffers. By being
present in the public square, Citizen Ninjas become citizen
stakeholders and avert being ruled by overlords.

Traditional Government

This triangle illustrates a traditional system of government that (with our consent) governs *for us*. Starting at the
bottom of the triangle, our greatest seat of power is at the
local level—town and city. Local agencies (city council, planning board, school board, etc.) are closest to the people.
The County is the next seat of power that manages regional
planning decisions that affect city and town jurisdictions.
This level of government is still considered local, as each
county agency (Board of Supervisors, Board
of Education, etc.)
has district repre-
sentatives who
live and work
close to their
constituents.
When Citizen Ninjas participate locally, we claim our
power, because our voice
can influence, contribute,
and impact public policy de-

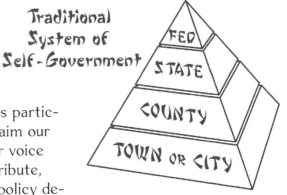

Traditional
System of
Self-Government

FED
STATE
COUNTY
TOWN or CITY

cisions. The further we move up the triangle, the less control government agencies should have over our local affairs. It is harder for us to have access and participate at the federal level, which is why local government is so crucial. The strength of our traditional system of government lies in the foundation of self-governance: active Citizen Ninjas working in partnership with their local elected public servants.

Top-Down Governance

By contrast, this triangle illustrates a government that governs *for us*. It is an over-weighted and top-heavy federal government that exerts so much influence and authority, self-government is squashed and diminished. Not only is it difficult to have a direct line of communication with Congress, distant federal agencies with **Top Down** increasing autonomy **Governance by** inject themselves into **Stakeholders** our lives and our local government by dispatching enforceable rules, laws, and regulations written by nameless bureaucrats and administrators. Because federal agencies are remote, this rulemaking has little accountability or transparency.

FEDERAL
STATE
PUBLIC PRIVATE PARTNERSHIP
COUNTY
TOWN OR CITY

Consider the couple who wanted to build a house on a lake in Idaho and after acquiring local permits, broke ground and started grading the land to build the foundation for their home. Within days, US Environmental Protection Agency (EPA) agents descended on the couple claiming that their lot was a federally protected wetland under the Clean Water Act. The EPA agents told the couple to restore the land back to its original condition or face up to $75,000/day fines. In addition, they were not allowed to pursue the EPA for redress of grievances until they had exhausted all administrative solutions.

The Clean Water Act is a good example of an EPA initiative that started out with good intentions and then was allowed by our Congressional legislators to morph into an overreaching regulatory machine. EPA and Army Corps of Engineers bureaucrats have stretched the definition of navigable waters to the point where almost any wet surface, bog, or swale, no matter how deep or how infrequently it is wet, falls under their rules. While public comments are allowed and often required when new regulations are proposed, the process is difficult because our voices get drowned out by scientific experts and large NPO/NGO stakeholders.

Stand Up to Power

By establishing professional, credible, working relationships with all your elected public servants and participating in government and politics, you can maintain self-government, a representative republic that governs *for* you with your consent and management instead of a centralized government that governs *over* you. Now that you understand why it is important to be involved in the civic process and you are equipped with your four Citizen Ninja powers (civic knowledge, self-restraint, self-assertion, self-reliance), you are ready to learn the tactics that will help you to stand up to dominant powers and face your public successfully.

9

Manage Emotions

Citizen Ninjas are adept at emotion regulation. We feel emotions intensely, but regulate them to achieve rational and objective discourse because "hot" emotions can curtail communication. Sensitive political dialogue can happen anywhere—with a neighbor, a relative, a stranger, an elected public servant, a school district superintendent; or with a group of people, like a community town hall, at the grocery store, a chamber of commerce meeting, a Little League Board, or a budget review committee meeting. Emotions can control us in negative ways. Citizen Ninjas channel emotions in positive ways to be more effective in the public square. Doing so doesn't come naturally—it must be learned.

What Spurs Action

Emotions are a remarkable human process that is hard-wired into the human system. We respond emotionally to surrounding environments, which drive and motivate us to act. Our instinctive sense of self-protection keeps us on alert, constantly assessing threats, without being aware of doing so. We behave the same way when we see someone else in danger. For example, when I see a child dash across the street in front of traffic I immediately fear for the child's safety, and that emotion drives me to quickly act to save the child. Without pondering the consequences; I just act.

This instinctive sense of self-protection focuses our attention when faced with danger, before a rational thought transmits in the brain, we instantly react. There are other situations that do not require quick action, allowing time for reflection. Before an exam, for example, students often feel anxiety, which tends to motivate them to study.

In the public square, reacting spontaneously to provocation is not as effective as responding thoughtfully. Citizen Ninjas channel emotional energy into productive action.

Injustice frequently stimulates fear and anger which might drive us to act in ways we've never done before, like participate in a protest or go to a school board meeting and make a public comment. Recall a time when you witnessed an injustice or were accosted by an aggressive person, but you did not speak up because you felt afraid. Maybe there was a moment when you spoke out in anger and wish you hadn't? Many of us feel intimidated to stand up for truth and justice because we are overwhelmed by strong emotions and unsure how to channel it into confidence when we engage in the public square.

For example, I was incensed by the violation of property rights through the Supreme Court's decision in Kelo v. City of New London, which motivated me to pay attention to politics. The unprecedented ruling in this eminent domain case supported the City of New London's action to take private property, transferring it from one private entity to another for the purpose of economic development. Specifically, a pharmaceutical company wanted to purchase land occupied by private homeowners and the City made the decision to kick the owners off their land by right of eminent domain because the pharmaceutical company would provide the city with more economic revenue than homeowners' property taxes.

As I was speaking disparagingly of the news of this outrage, my husband said to me: "Instead of ranting, why don't you go and do something about it?!!" My husband's challenge hit home. This was an abuse of the government's right to take private property, and the US Supreme Court approved it! I suddenly felt driven to speak up.

Yet, I was afraid of sharing my opinion in public for fear of be-

COMMON FEARS

Mind Going Blank
Retaliation
Lack of Knowledge
Stage Fright
Being Bullied

Loss of Friendships
Being Labeled
Making a Mistake
Loss of Respect
Rejection

ing bullied and criticized. Fear and anger can be paralyzing. People wanting to become Citizen Ninjas are often paralyzed by strong emotions like fear and anger. I've witnessed citizens at town hall meetings get up and scream, cry, bully, and use sarcasm to communicate their dissatisfaction and pain. Others won't speak up at all. I've known parents who so fear retaliation by the Superintendent, they won't attend school board meetings to protect their kids from potential unfair treatment by a coach, teacher, or school administrator. By contrast, Citizen Ninjas examine their fears and anger to redirect them.

Rise Above Fear

Fear alerts us to physical and emotional danger. Our re-action to fear whether it is real or perceived is to fight or flee. Heeding fear is fundamental to our survival. When afraid we experience physical sensations that we cannot seem to control: senses heighten, wits sharpen as we become intensely aware of the surroundings. We instinctively run away or fight.

Often we fear situations that are not actually life threatening, such as speaking in public because our mind does not distinguish between real and perceived life threatening situations. André, for example, suffers from seizures and benefits from using medical marijuana. At a golf tournament, the topic of Colorado's new marijuana use laws came up and the general consensus by the foursome was that the laws would negatively impact the State. André, who has not learned the Citizen Ninja way, was afraid he would lose the group's respect if he revealed his medicinal use of marijuana—so he stayed silent.

Inner Talk

Some people fear losing friendships, being labeled, bullied, or rejected. Others have stage fright, fearing their mind will go blank, or they will make a mistake. For example, at a social gathering Juan told himself: "With all the liberals here I'll be ridiculed and rejected if I voice my views." Imagining being ridiculed and rejected are triggers that set off hardwired protective programs of fight or flight—anger or withdrawal.

Citizen Ninjas practice empowered inner talk. Instead of allowing fear and anger to control you, calm yourself by "reframing"—redefining—how you think or talk to yourself about what is happening. For example, Juan might think—inner talk—about the gathering: "My liberal colleagues disagree with my views, but I have clear reasons for supporting the conservative's position so I can speak up."

Negative inner thoughts about failure, like "They're all looking at me and thinking that I'm an idiot" before delivering a public comment at a water board meeting will likely trigger anxiety. By rewriting the words to be positive without the trigger, such as "When I speak the facts slowly, I will make a strong impression." Juan will feel more in control and calm when delivering his comments.

Perceptions

When I started public speaking, I was afraid of being marginalized and bullied. I had seen and heard examples of spokespersons being bullied on national television and syndicated radio. I worried I wouldn't be able to stand up to verbal attacks and hostility. I feared losing my train of thought, not having all the facts, and making mistakes. While examining these fears, I found it interesting that my initial reaction was similar to how I feel when I perceive I might be in a threatening situation—my surroundings come into sharp focus, my body tenses, my pulse quickens, my eyes scan the scene, and I become acutely aware of sound.

Speaking in public, which is the most common fear among adults, "feels" threatening, but it is not a threat to survival, as encountering a thug brandishing a weapon would be. Nevertheless, contemplating speaking up to a domineering person, for example, triggers the fight-or-flight "program" and the body then responds as if we were actually facing a thug in a dark alley or being chased by a junk yard guard dog—with panic, dry mouth, shaking, sweating, stuttering, thumping heartbeat, wet palms, and the desire to turn away. To quell this instinctive reaction, Citizen Ninjas pause and "reframe"—redefine—what is happening to describe it to oneself in non-threatening ways. When you tell yourself with your inner talk that you are in danger of being ridiculed, for example. This knee-jerk-like response can be avoided by changing the words of your inner talk, by redefining events to not be "threatening" and "dangerous", rather you might "tell yourself" that you face a challenge, for example. When you become adept at redefining perils as challenges, you gain considerable control over your reactivity. Then you can proceed using Citizen Ninja tactics, while employing empowered inner talk to manage your instinctive fear.

A hot temper is the soil of remorse.

AMBROSE BIERCE
19th c. author

Manage Anger

Participating in government and political process can be provocative. If all people agreed with every ideology, policy and rule, there would be no need to act. When situated in a charged setting, citizens can be flooded with emotions, especially anger. Anger will often provoke us to either speak out emotionally or to not speak out at all. Known for his satirical lexicon, *The Devil's Dictionary*, Ambrose Bierce said: "Speak when you are angry and you will make the best speech you will ever regret." Anger is an emotion many of us find challenging to control, and how we react to it merits our examination. The American Psychological Association (APA) suggests we control our anger before it controls us. The APA describes anger as a completely normal, usually healthy, human emotion, except when it gets out of control.

Dirk, who does not know the Citizen Ninja way, was angry about the news that veterans would be permitted to carry a concealed handgun in the wake of the most recent shooting at a recruiting station in his town. In a Letter to the Editor, Dirk insulted vets by claiming they were all victims of post-traumatic stress and the public should not trust their judgment. He immediately regretted his outburst when the community flooded the airwaves with angry reactions and marginalized him as a "vet hater." The words we say and our ensuing actions can be destructive and lead to problems. Lashing out angrily is not an effective way to have productive discourse on an issue.

Channel Anger into Passion

Mismanaged anger can grow into rage. Rage is so powerful that it can be terrifying. Citizen Ninjas wield the power of self-restraint and maintain composure regardless of the intensity of the anger. Consider Citizen Ninja Meiling. She was upset when she found out that her eight-year old daughter's eyes were becoming increasingly myopic and that their condition might be due to a technology program that her daughter's elementary school had implemented one year earlier. The program requires the daily use of iPads™ by the children and she worried the notepads were damaging her daughter's vision.

Anger, like fear and anxiety, is triggered not by events, but what we tell ourself about events. If in Meiling's inner talk she accused the school of being irresponsible and endagering her child, she would be angry—perhaps too angry—to deal with the issue effectively.

Instead of storming into the principal's office and accusing him of being irresponsible, Meiling thought about inner talk—how she might gather facts to develop a strong case against the use of iPads™. She decided to conduct an informal survey to see if other children in her daughter's grade had also been diagnosed with myopia. Meiling found that some parents reported the same condition—eyes that had normal vision were becoming nearsighted. This prompted Meiling and a couple of other parents to attend a school board meeting where, armed with facts and personal anecdotes, they requested the board form a task force to study the health effects of iPads™ in the classroom on children in elementary schools. The school board was not persuaded, so Meiling and her new colleagues increased their research and started educating other parents about the negative impacts technology might be having on young kids. Their passion for this cause inspired activity that brought increased community attention. Eventually, enough people were alarmed that the district finally acquiesced and formed a task force to study the risks of the technology program.

When you are angry about something, become a Citizen Ninja and channel your anger into passion, which empowers you and drives your commitment to the cause. When you *react* in anger to provocation and goading, you diminish your influence and power to engage in civil discourse and effect change. By contrast, when you *respond* with passion, you build trust and respect. Unchecked anger is toxic and usually dissuades people from rallying around your cause; passion, on the other hand, is what moves people in a positive way. In Citizen Ninja Meiling's case, her approach was to solve the problem, not to point fingers and discredit the principal, the district, or the trustees through personal attack campaigns. Consequently, people rallied around her in support of the cause.

Be Mindful

The first step to overcoming anger and other disruptive emotions is to become aware of the inner talk that triggers anger. When you are mindful and listen to what you tell yourself, you can rewrite negative scripts that trigger debilitating emotions. A good way to do this is to rethink situations from your past and your reaction to them.

Try this: on a sheet of paper, list several situations from the past when you had a strong opinion on an issue but avoided revealing your thoughts to a neighbor, a friend, or a family member. When you have several items on your list, select one and, with your eyes closed, relive it in your mind's eye, while dispassionately watching yourself. Don't judge yourself; instead simply observe yourself in the situation.

Notice how you feel as you relive the interaction and rate your feeling on a scale of 1-5, with 1 being very comfortable and 5 being extremely uncomfortable.

Now relive the event again in your mind and listen carefully to your inner talk—what specifically did you say to yourself about events? What specific *words* did you use to talk to yourself just before and during the encounter? The words can be fleeting, so observe closely. Write down the specific words you were thinking—that is, saying to yourself.

Suppose, for example, that you told yourself, "Janice is so smart—she will think that I'm uninformed and silly if I voice my opinion." Negative words such as these are triggers that set off our hard-wired survival programs. On an unconscious level this sort of "snap analysis" makes us think that being rejected by Janice is tantamount to be thrown out of the tribe to starve! Of course Janice's condescending opinion is actually not life threatening, but to your "primitive brain," it is a kind of death sentence—to which you responded by keeping your acceptable views hidden so as to avoid the danger.

The way Citizen Ninjas rewrite this primitive life-or-death response program when it comes up inappropriately is by rewriting words that trigger anxiety and withdrawal—changing them into neutral, or, better, empowering words. In this rewriting you redefine the situation so as to not be frightening. For example, you might rewrite what you told yourself about the encounter with Janice as: "Janice can be snarky but I have facts and that stumps her." These words trigger feelings of confidence and coolness.

Examine the words you used to talk to yourself about the practice event and rewrite them to remove fear triggers and to state facts. Now close your eyes again and, while observing how you feel, relive the same experience— this time purposefully saying the rewritten words: "I have the facts and facts stump Janice." Let the scenario run in your mind to its natural conclusion with the new inner talk, imagining that Janice would have listened and nodded, even if grumpily. Now go back to the Comfort/Discomfort scale of 1-5 and rate how you feel when saying the new script. How does the second rating compare to the first? If you're like most people, you will find yourself more comfortable and less anxious with the empowered inner talk—and will be able, in future encounters, to be a more effective Citizen Ninja.

Mind Training

Ninja warriors practice Ninjutsu, the art of the ninja, to train the mind to perceive the present moment accurately in order to assess future perceptions of reality. For us as Citizen Ninjas, this means staying aware of our emotions and our environment. We teach ourselves to distinguish perceived danger from real danger, and we make deliberate choices about whether to engage or not. We rarely find ourselves in situations where we have to react to provocation, because Citizen Ninjas take the time to be aware and to determine how to respond appropriately, rather than with a knee-jerk reaction that will antagonize others and fail to promote the civil discourse that we seek. Among the tactics we use to evaluate a situation and decide how to handle it, are *zones of awareness, identifying opportunities, and pegging*. We will now explore each of these in detail.

10

Zones of Awareness

C itizen Ninjas operate in well-defined *Zones of Awareness.* Zones are situations we encounter on a daily basis. Being mindful of zones helps to spot opportunities for municipal engagement and political discourse. Employing Zones of Awareness helps Citizen Ninjas be proactive conversationalists instead of reactive ones.

I developed this tactic from my eighteen-year-old daughter's self-defense instructor who was teaching, Emma, special techniques prior to her solo trip to Europe. Before he began teaching her the evasive moves to use against an assailant, he emphasized the benefits of employing alert levels.

Alert Levels

There are three alert levels: *condition white, condition yellow,* and *condition red.* Most people wander about daily in a relaxed state or what Emma's instructor called: condition white. People would be safer if they employed a condition yellow state of mind, which is a vigilant mind-set that scans and identifies potentially dangerous areas and prepares the person to be ready for condition red—the attack.

Predators look for people who are not paying attention to their surroundings—condition white—people who are texting with their head down, wearing headphones, or talking with someone, for example. Predators count on the element of surprise to have the upper hand in an attack. If we are out in the streets with a condition white mind set when it should be in condition yellow, then we are a target. Emma's instructor taught us to tuck our cell phone back in our purse or pocket, put our head on a swivel, and think proactively. Asking ourselves questions like: What kind of vehicle is parked next to mine? Is there someone loitering around the area I am headed to, should I get on the elevator with this person? Am I being followed? We realized the only way to be ready for an attack (condition red) is if we had a condition yellow mind-set.

If we are aware of our surroundings and are thinking proactively, we radically decrease our chances of becoming a victim. If we are attacked despite being prepared, then we are ready to defend ourselves and that alone is enough to thwart the attack. Predators assume we are unprepared to defend ourselves.

Emma learned that being in condition white while she was traveling solo, left her vulnerable and if she was going to avoid condition red situations, she was better off traveling with a condition yellow mind-set.

Zones of Awareness

I've adapted the self-defense alert levels to the Citizen Ninja way. To better respond to uncomfortable situations or provocations, Citizen Ninjas employ Zones of Awareness: *Rest, Assess,* and *Engage* Zones. Think of a Zone as a place. For example, home is generally a peaceful and safe

place. It is an environment where you can be yourself without fear of judgment. Home is an example of a Rest Zone.

Rest Zone

To Citizen Ninjas, the Rest Zone is a place where opinions and ideas are formulated and shared with loved ones. It is a place where you can be at rest; where your mind is not seeking opportunities for municipal engagement. For example, Citizen Ninja Micah mulls over political issues with his wife before discussing them with his co-workers. Micah finds that developing some clarity ahead of time in the Rest Zone helps him to have thoughtful, civil political discourse when he and his co-workers disagree.

Assess Zone

As you leave the Rest Zone, shift your mind-set to the *Assess Zone*. The Assess Zone is where Citizen Ninjas are alert, scanning and identifying opportunities to engage in political discourse. When you are out and about in your community, your Assess Zone focus actively evaluates the environment, people, and sounds that surround you.

The natural state of being aware and alert when out in the public realm is like being in condition yellow. You are situationally aware, which helps you make quick decisions when unexpected situations arise, such as when a car makes a sudden illegal U-turn while you are crossing the road.

Alternatively, imagine being at the grocery store. While shopping for items, you assess products and make choices about what to put into your cart; you keep an eye on your cart as you walk about and you are cautious rounding the aisle corner to avoid bumping into someone. You are aware of your  environment—shoppers, clerks, products, sounds, and space. Suppose you see someone you know at the end of the aisle. Based on past experience with this person, you make a quick decision: walk the other way or say hello? When choosing to say hello, you enter the *Engage Zone.*

Engage Zone

Imagine being in the Rest Zone at the grocery store, unaware of the surroundings, suddenly you look up and someone is standing right in front of you. This is the moment when you must engage. If you know and like the person, the moment is enjoyable, but if you have issues with the person, or it is a stranger, the moment can be awkward.

The Engage Zone is easier to manage when aware of your surroundings, and more difficult when taken by surprise if in the Rest Zone. Facing the public successfully requires Citizen Ninjas to shift Zones quickly to what is appropriate for the situation. Being in the Rest Zone when it would be better to be in the Assess Zone can lead to uncomfortable dialogue. Encounters are less awkward when you can *respond* to a situation rather than *reacting* to it. Reactions happen when you are unprepared (Rest Zone) so you react emotionally rather than responding thoughtfully.

Switch Zones

Consider what happened when Ima, who has not learned the Citizen Ninja way, interacted with someone at a party in the Rest Zone when her mind-set should have been in the Assess Zone.

Ima and her husband were relaxed at a wine tasting party in a nearby neighborhood, enjoying the food. On the way into the house for dessert, Trish, another guest, asked how her remodeling was going. Somehow that neutral question landed their conversation on property rights issues. The tone of their dialogue was civil until Trish challenged Ima's definition of property rights. "Well, Ima,"

Trish categorically stated: "I believe that animals have rights too and should be protected from too much human development and population growth."

Ima's inner voice immediately bellowed: "Whoa!!!" as she wondered how they went from a conversation about re-modeling her den to a tense argument about animal rights and human overpopulation in under three minutes. She felt unprepared to discuss the issues. Instead of responding like a Citizen Ninja with: "Well, that would be a great conversation for another time. Let's have coffee next week!" She reacted in astonishment and blurted out: "What?! Are you placing animal rights over the rights of humans to own property?!"

With those clumsy words, Ima stepped away feeling terrible—not because Trish and Ima had divergent opinions (there's nothing wrong with that), but because Ima wished she had reacted less defensively. Had Ima been a Citizen Ninja, she would have switched her Rest Zone mind-set to the Assess Zone as Trish started to direct the conversation toward property rights. When Trish declared her beliefs, Ima would have been more prepared for the Engage Zone. By suggesting they meet for coffee the following week, she would have bought herself time to organize her thoughts on animal rights.

Be Deliberate

The Engage Zone is the moment when you decide to either respond thoughtfully to a statement like Trish's or initiate a different topic of discussion. In a public setting, the Assess Zone is crucial,

because deliberate, situational awareness enables Citizen Ninjas to choose whether or not to speak.

Making a deliberate choice to proceed or to not proceed into the Engage Zone puts you in control of the encounter. Like ninja warriors, Citizen Ninjas are prepared for multiple situations and events. Once you engage, your four Citizen Ninja powers are activated. Rely on the power of *civic knowledge* to develop strategies that help analyze situations, environments, or people. The power of *self-restraint* helps to have meaningful dialogues that maintain credibility. *Self-assertion* is the power that encourages you to engage when it's appropriate, and the power of *self-reliance* reminds you that Citizen Ninjas don't wait for others to act or speak. When you are in charge, you have more confidence.

Spotting Opportunities

The Zones of Awareness model affords time to respond to situations. It helps identify opportunities for municipal engagement or political discourse. Many opportunities to speak are scheduled, like the monthly planning board meeting or the League of Women Voters luncheon. Other opportunities are premeditated, like planning to speak to parents about a bullying incident in a school parking lot or talking politics at the barber shop. Sometimes opportunities to speak happen unexpectedly, as in Ima's example. If your mind-set is operating in the proper zone, opportunities to speak become easier to spot and to manage. In the next chapter, we will look at the many different ways to engage in your community.

11

Civic Engagement

Daily life is filled with ways that lead Citizen Ninjas to community engagement and political discourse. Our municipal activity is measured by three different types of engagement: civic, electoral, and political. In the next three chapters, we will learn how Citizen Ninjas are participating in each of these areas of engagement.

Civic engagement includes both community and municipal activities. Each activity is rated from less intensive to more intensive, so if you don't have any activism experience, I recommend choosing activities that match your comfort level, talents, and interests. As you gain experience and develop skills, you can venture into more challenging opportunities. The discussion here is brief and meant to pique your interest! As you read through the examples in each category, jot down on a sheet of paper activities you may be willing to try.

Community Volunteering

Freely offering our skills and time fosters quality of life in the community. Citizen Ninjas volunteer to be youth sports coaches, organize the yearly 4th of July parade, join the local Friends of the Library or Performing Arts Center, work in the District as an election poll worker, contribute time to the PTA, or help clean up trash along a favorite biking trail. Untold numbers of Citizen Ninjas work to clean up their neighborhoods without recognition. They do it because there's a mess that needs to be cleaned up, or a broken fence that needs fixing.

Community volunteer opportunities are typically short-term and do not require full-time commitment. As a Citizen Ninja volunteer, you can invest as much time as your schedule allows, making the intensity of this activity low to moderate or, if you wish, moderate to high.

Active Membership

Belonging to a political club or league is a social way for Citizen Ninjas to stay informed—and fun! But it is important to be an *active* member. Too often, people shy away from leadership positions, leaving the job to others. A diversity of leadership allows for changes in vision and checks the organization against internal bias and corruption. Groups like the League of Women Voters, Young Democrats of America, Federation of Republican Women, Tea Party, building trade associations, Chambers of Commerce, Children's Hospital Auxiliary, Oathkeepers, Realtor's Association, Kiwanis, and Lion's Club are all opportunities for engagement.

Civic group activity only requires a little effort when starting off as just a member. As you become more involved and work your way into leadership positions the intensity of activity will increase. For example, Citizen Ninja Delores started off as a casual member of Children's Hospital Auxiliary (CHAUX). She attended the monthly meetings and participated in two annual fundraisers. As she became more comfortable with the organization and the members, her commitment increased. Delores joined the annual gala fundraiser committee, then chaired the event the following year. Her role as membership chair eventually brought her the nomination for CHAUX president.

Citizen Ninjas recognize the importance of being active members, and when you step up and lead, you help to perpetuate the life of an organization. The intensity of this activity may begin as low to moderate, but can become moderate to high over time.

Volunteering for Leadership Roles

Membership on many government boards do not require a vote by the people. Citizen Ninjas only need apply to be considered for an appointment. When selected, the position keeps you informed and ensures your voice is heard when important matters are discussed. Appointed committee positions might include budget review, curriculum review, parks and recreation, traffic safety, and community services. Appointed board and commission positions might include development and planning, environmental impacts, water conservation, irriga-tion districts, natural resources, port authority and so on.

With many appointments, there is ethics training on fair political practices. The intensity of this activity is low to moderate, and before handing in an application, consider calling the government agen-cy to enquire about the commitment parameters of the position.

Grassroots Organizing

Local activism is a high-impact way for Citizen Ninjas to mobilize a community for a cause. It is impactful because the cause is generated by the needs of the people and not promoted by special interest groups or the government acting alone. For example, a Citizen Ninja who was a com-munity services director in San Juan Islands, Washington, organized and founded a non-profit preschool when budget cuts forced the only preschool in town to close. In Phila-delphia, a group of Citizen Ninjas, frustrated by the lack of grants available to small or less-known nonprofits, rallied 100 women to donate $1,000 each to create a substantial $100,000 grant. They created a competitive grant applica-tion process and every member voted among five finalists.

This grassroots organization now boasts over 300 members and has granted $1,645,000 in seven years.

To initiate a cause, Citizen Ninjas might start by reaching out to the City to determine interest. Consider Citizen Ninja Jim, a veteran who wanted to see a war memorial erected to recognize the several hundred local vets who had died and served since the founding of the town. He approached the City Council, which supported the effort. It took over a year, but working with City staff, Council, and the support of the community, Jim succeeded. Grassroots organizing is an intensive activity and Citizen Ninjas who are interested in running a campaign for office in the future often start this way.

Elected Public Servant

Every two years there is an election—unless a special election is convened. In all regions across America there are thousands of positions available collectively. These positions are divided into national, state, county, and local districts. Running a campaign is an intensive activity, but if you've been actively engaging in the political process, being a candidate is a logical next step, especially if there is an objectionable incumbent or an open seat. Citizen Ninja candidates invest time in fundraising and get-out-the-vote activities such as precinct walking and speaking at local forums and service organizations. Name recognition and a volunteer track record go a long way with voters, so early, consistent involvement within the community is important.

It is remarkable that every year there are hundreds of open seats that draw no candidates or go unchallenged. Seats that do not draw any candidates are filled by appointment. This is a great opportunity for Citizen Ninjas! After an election, check with city hall or the school district if there are any open seats that you can apply for. Another great opportunity for Citizen Ninjas are seats that go unchallenged. These seats are either incumbent seats or open ones, meaning the incumbent's term is up and he or she is choosing not to run again. Some examples of these include school board, community college trustee, planning, water, and public utility boards, fire protection, and superior court judges. Just before the filing deadline check with your local registrar of voters which seats are still open. If there is no one running, you pay the fee to be on the ballot and run a campaign that focuses mainly on voter outreach with some fundraising.

12

Electoral Engagement

Electoral engagement means participating in elections and campaigns for election known as Get Out the Vote (GOTV). If you are eighteen years of age and a citizen of the US, you are eligible to vote. Voting is a fundamental civic right and your experience at the voting booth should always be a positive experience without pressure or intimidation to vote for one candidate over another. Beyond voting, electoral engagement includes helping others register to vote, precinct walking which involves walking neighborhoods to share campaign literature, or introducing preferred candidates to your family, friends, or community by hosting a candidate forum.

Choose activities to match your comfort level, talents, and interests. Remember to jot down activities you already participate in on a sheet of paper and then make a list of the ones you would be willing to try.

Vote Regularly

One of our most cherished rights is the freedom to vote for candidates of our choice. Voting is a citizen's primary obligation and Citizen Ninjas vote in every election. Our vote counts and that should never be underestimated. Consider the city council candidate who won by *two* votes in a highly contested recount in Chula Vista, a city in southern Californiab. If three citizens had not voted, the incumbent would have won.

To ensure that your vote counts, it takes little effort to make sure your address is current with the registrar of voters so you don't have to ask for a provisional ballot on Election Day. When voting by absentee ballot make sure you mail it before the deadline. Absentee ballots that are walked-in to the precinct on Election Day are not counted until after thepolling station election is over. Voting in person is the best way to counter voter fraud.

Volunteer to Register Voters

Both Democrat and Republican organizations as well as many otheres work to register voters. A satisfying experience for Citizen Ninjas is to register new US citizens to vote.

The first time I worked a registration booth at a new US citizens' ceremony people from many different countries, speaking different languages were clutching their certificates. One older Hispanic man asked me in broken English if he could register to vote. Because I speak Spanish, I was able to assist him. I took him to the booth and sat down. As I translated line by line, he filled in the card. When he was done, he stood up, shook my hand, tipped his hat, smiled broadly and thanked me. I felt that I made a difference.

Invest as much time in registering voters as your schedule allows, making the intensity of this activity low to moderate.

Display Campaign Literature

Campaign literature is printed in many forms and includes signs, buttons, bumper stickers, and pamphlets. Putting a campaign sign on your front lawn, wearing a pin, or displaying a bumper sticker are easy indirect ways for you as a Citizen Ninja to declare your support for a candidate or proposition without having to tell people directly. This activity requires little effort: all you have to do is contact the campaign headquarters and request an assortment of campaign paraphernalia, and the candidate's staff is happy to swing by and deliver it.

Host a Candidate Forum

A candidate forum is a meeting hosted by an organiza-tion that seeks to educate the public about the candidates running for office. Generally, all candidates are invited to come to the forum to deliver a brief introduction and say what they hope to accomplish on the community's behalf if elected to office. At the end of the forum, the candidates are usually available for a meet and greet.

Hosting a forum is an excellent way for Citizen Ninjas to bring together candidates and their constituents. The intensity of this activity is moderate—it requires you to find a location for the event, send invitations to the candidates and the public, set up chairs and a PA system, and arrange for some refreshments. For the public, a candidate forum may be the only opportunity to meet candidates and ask questions.

Walk Precincts

Walking the neighborhoods with a candidate is a powerful way for Citizen Ninjas to reach an electorate.
It's a fun activity to do with a group of people. The intensity levels range from moderate to high depending on your commitment level. You may choose to walk neighborhoods for only one day, or opt for once a week for the duration of the cam-paign.

Most candidates focus on high propensity voters from their own political party as well as voters who are de-clined-to-state and whose vote is therefore considered "up for grabs." Focusing on those constituents makes the process more enjoyable and less unpredictable because when you knock on the door, you can expect to be speaking to like-minded or open-minded individuals.

Precinct walking is a great mechanism for voter outreach. Because it is basically "cold calling" it can be an intimidating activity for budding Citizen Ninjas. However, knowing the candidate's talking points and sharing personal stories about why you support the candidate makes it easier—and good practice for speaking up.

13

Political Engagement

The Political category is where Citizen Ninjas demonstrate passion for self-government, which is what politics should be about. Giving a public comment at a local school board meeting, organizing a rally in support of or in protest to an issue, or meeting with elected and non-elected public servants are all ways to participate in the political dimension. These types of actions effect the change you are promoting because they are grassroots activities prompted by citizens rather than special interest groups that are pushing their own agenda. Tools like flyering (posting or handing out leaflets), letters to the editor, and speaking at the public mic at a PTA meeting, a rally, or council meeting will help you communicate your political message.

As with the Civic and Electoral categories, each activity is rated as less intensive to moderate to very intensive. As you gain experience and develop your skills, you can venture into more challenging opportunities. The information provided is meant to pique your interest! As before, jot down the activities you already participate in on a sheet of paper and then make a list of the ones you would be willing to try.

Post Flyers

Many Citizen Ninjas find posting flyers an effective and inexpensive way to communicate a message on a

particular issue to the public. There are many traditional ways to flyer, like putting leaflets on car windshields in
parking lots or handing them out in a public place, like the
entrance to a grocery store. Citizen Ninja Anna puts flyers
into magazines whenever she goes to an appointment and
must sit in the waiting room. While she is waiting, Anna
inserts flyers in the magazines. This is low to moderate
intensity activism with productive outreach.

Write Letters to the Editor

Writing letters to the editor to voice your opinion or respond to a published article is effective to reach both local
and national public audiences as well as legislators and policy
makers. To increase your chance of being published, make
your statements short, to the point, relevant, and factual.
Newspapers and magazines provide guidelines for accep-
tance, which makes this a low to moderate intensity activity.

Participate in a Rally

Participating in peaceful rallies is a great way for Citizen
Ninjas to communicate their message to a large and diverse
group of individuals. Because a rally is generally made up of
a large number of people, participants are not singled out
and so feel less intimidated about voicing opinions.

   If there is a cause you strongly support, a quick search
on the Internet or social media will inform you if there are
any events you can participate in. You can identify the type
of gathering by the title: rally, protest, or demonstration.
Rallies tend to be events that energize a base. For example,
a group might organize a rally to support the candidate of
their choice while she is in town for a fundraiser. *Protests*
are generally organized to register opposition regarding a
public issue. For example, a group might gather to protest a
recent decision by the courts. Citizens *demonstrate* to communicate a viewpoint as it relates to political, economic, or

social matters. For example, there might be a demonstration in front of the local library to show support for keeping the facility open despite budget cuts.

Depending on the size and duration of the event, the intensity level of this activity is moderate to high. Depending on how involved you want to be, you may invite friends to join you, create a sign or banner, carpool to combine resources, bring water and snacks, wear appropriate gear depending on the weather, and wear comfortable shoes.

Organize a Rally

Organizing a rally, protest, or demonstration is a highly intensive activity, but the benefit of being the host gives Citizen Ninjas greater control over the event. Any assembly that energizes like-minded supporters or communicates grievances can significantly impact your local communities and gain potential media attention.

• Plan Ahead!

Many municipalities require permits to gather in public spaces and event insurance may also be necessary. Several weeks in advance of your event, call city hall to obtain everything you need to be in compliance. When selecting your venue, keep in mind parking and bathroom facilities as well as the size of the venue. If you anticipate a small assembly, choose a smaller venue—a larger one would only make the group look smaller. To ensure the safety of your assembly, identify people in the group who can act as security in case of violent disruptors.

• Spread the Word!

When the details of your event are settled, invite elected public servants and the media. The goal is to reach as many people as possible, and rallies are an opportunity for maximum exposure. To get the word out, publicize the event on social media and email networks, and send out a press release.

• Stay on Message!

On the day of the event, bring plenty of signage that specifies your message. To amplify your voice, consider using a bullhorn, or orchestrate chants as a powerful means to swell the voice of the assembly. If the TV cameras are rolling, be prepared with talking points, and if the media do not show up, capture the event and people's statements on camera to share on social media.

• Clean up!

If you plan on hosting more rallies in the future, it behooves you to leave the venue the way you found it when your event is over. The last impression should be a positive one.

Write a Resolution

A resolution is a formal statement of an organization's position on a topic or policy. Resolutions are written using a specific format that includes a heading, "whereas..." statements, and "therefore be it resolved..." statements. This is a moderate-to-high intensity activity, because writing these takes some effort and knowledge, and expertise on an issue. But it is a valuable use of your time and energy. A quick search on the Internet about how to write them is all it takes to create the proper format.

Citizen Ninjas write and submit resolutions to a variety of governmental and non-governmental organizations. For example, several years back more than forty towns in New Hampshire approved a resolution calling on the Legislature to allow a vote on the definition of marriage. And at one point, in Texas, more than 100 school districts passed a resolution saying that high-stakes standardized tests were "strangling" public schools. Resolutions are a powerful tool, because they reflect the resolve of the people. There is power in numbers.

Contact Officials

Some people contact elected public servants only when concerned with a particular issue or when they disagree with the result of a vote by a board. By contrast, Citizen Ninjas routinely contact officials before votes are cast to chat about issues in the City or School District or to convey approval of a decision the Council has made, for example. As a result, elected public servants are more inclined to listen to Citizen Ninjas in the future.

Make it your goal to contact elected public servants once a quarter by phone or email. Schedule a time to meet for coffee to chat about things that are going on and ask if there is anything you can do to support their work. Officials appreciate the attention and like knowing citizens care about what is going on in the community. Participating in this activity is of moderate intensity, and it is what facilitates Citizen Ninja appointments to a city's Budget Review or Parks and Recreation Committee, for example.

Attend a Public Meeting

One of the best ways to stay informed about the current issues, plans, and challenges in your community is to attend a local city council or school board meeting.

When you show up at these meetings, you are conveying to the council or board that you care about the community. Often public meetings are streamed live or are recorded for later viewing, which enables the community to stay informed when unable to attend the meeting. Low intensity is to read the agenda of an upcoming meeting so that you know what the governing board will be discussing. The next level of effort is to attend meetings regularly, like once a month. Intensity increases when you deliver a public comment at the designated microphone.

Speak at Public Mic

Citizen Ninjas understand the importance of walking up to the public mic to register themselves as in favor of or opposition to an agenda item. An agenda is a list of items to be discussed at a meeting. An agenda item is a topic or issue brought before a board or council for their consideration and public deliberation. Local government is structured so that any citizen can contribute an opinion and relevant fact finding on an agenda item, in public, to a governing agency, its staff, the media, and the community. Citizens may also bring up a topic that is not on the published agenda; this is called a non-agenda item.

The importance of participating in this more-intensive activity cannot be understated. Elected public servants, who govern with the consent of the public, cannot read citizens' minds—that is the purpose of the public comment. Standing at the podium, reading your statement into the mic is your opportunity to tell the governing board sitting behind the dais—the raised platform where groups typically sit during meetings—that you agree or disagree with the proposal being discussed. This is also a chance to make a public announcement about an upcoming event, or share grievances or praise. To raise your comfort level before going up to the podium, follow these Citizen Ninja steps.

• Steps for Making a Public Comment

Suppose you read the agenda of an upcoming City Council meeting on the City website and there's an agenda item that concerns you. Before the meeting, prepare a statement that takes less than two to three minutes to read. A typical statement includes a greeting, an introduction to the issue, your view on the matter, and a proposed solution.

Arrive fifteen minutes early so that you have time to fill out the public comment card, which is generally placed next to the printed agenda at the entrance to the meeting room. There will be a place on the card to indicate you wish to speak on an agenda or a non-agenda item. If you are addressing an agenda item, write the agenda item reference number located on the meeting agenda. Hand the card over to the clerk, who is usually seated up at the dais.

When your name is called, go to the podium and adjust the microphone so you can be heard. You will be given two to three minutes to deliver your comment. Usually there is a timer that shows how much time you have left. Read your prepared statement slowly and clearly into the microphone. Rarely will the Council or Board respond to your statement.

To have an interaction with the Council or Board, submit a request to the clerk ten days prior to the meeting to be on the agenda. Being on the agenda means your issue is on the list of items to be discussed at the meeting. This gives you more time to address the governing board or council, and other speakers can join you. PowerPoint™ slides and hand-outs are permitted when you are on the agenda, and they too become a permanent part of the minutes—which is beneficial because it puts the governing body on official notice about the issue you addressed.

I was nervous the first time I made a public comment, but after observing others, I knew I didn't have to be a loquacious orator to communicate my message. I observed that reading a direct, clear, and concise message was an effective way to register my opinion. The surprising outcome from my first experience was that two Council Members contacted me to thank me for participating in the meeting. Being politically engaged—showing up and speaking—conveys that you care about the community.

14

Opportunities to Engage

Community engagement in all three categories (civic, electoral, and political) supports a strong and healthy representative self-government—citizens working with each other and with their elected public servants. But Citizen Ninjas are not only committed to participating in municipal activities. We are also intent on finding formal and informal political discourse opportunities with our family, friends, neighbors, co-workers, and members of the public.

Opportunities for political discourse are found about town and at social gatherings. The idea is to proactively engage people in civil political discourse. We shouldn't expect to change people's minds, it is simply to encourage dialogue about government and politics. There are an endless number of situations that provide openings for us to ask questions and share our facts or opinions! Using our four Citizen Ninja powers and Zones of Awareness, we Citizen Ninjas identify opportunities for engagement and make choices whether or not to speak or take part. The more we operate in the *assess zone*, the more opportunities we will spot. Then, all that is required is for us to decide whether or not we feel comfortable to engage and speak.

Daily, Weekly, Monthly

Daily, weekly, or monthly opportunities for political discourse in our community are endless. We might seize an
opportunity to speak with someone about the pros and
cons of city mandated minimum wage increases while shopping at Walmart, or we might let people know about the
city's proposed community gardens project while shopping
at the local Farmer's Market. Citizen Ninja Erica likes to
draw people into newspaper-headline chats while standing
in lines at coffee shops, pharmacies, and grocery stores;
Citizen Ninja Daron finds it interesting to talk to people in
waiting rooms if they're up to it. About town there are op-
portunities at retail shops, the DMV, post office, gas stations, school parking lots, banks, malls, nail salon, shooting range, or

community center classes.
Social gatherings at senior centers, private homes, sport-
ing events, family dinners, card/chess/poker games, work
break rooms, churches, and exercise classes all present opportunities to engage in political discourse with the public.

A favorite opportunity is my monthly visit to the hair
salon. Like me, my hair stylist loves to chat about current
issues. Since the hair salon is boisterous and a place where
people speak loudly, it gives us a chance to speak plainly
about politics. It is also an opportunity for me to share
facts with others while seeming to be absorbed in just
a two-way conversation. People around us can't help but
overhear what we are talking about, so a degree of aware-

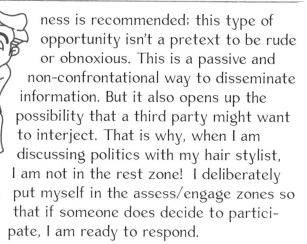

ness is recommended; this type of opportunity isn't a pretext to be rude or obnoxious. This is a passive and non-confrontational way to disseminate information. But it also opens up the possibility that a third party might want to interject. That is why, when I am discussing politics with my hair stylist, I am not in the rest zone! I deliberately put myself in the assess/engage zones so that if someone does decide to partici-pate, I am ready to respond.

Be Selective

It is important that Citizen Ninjas assess opportunities before they decide to speak. Just because we see opportu-nities does not mean we have to engage every time. That would be exhausting! Engaging others takes energy, so we have to pace ourselves and pick the opportunities that we perceive to be the most fruitful.

We can judge worthwhile opportunities by quickly assessing the amount of time there is to engage, the top-ic, and the type of venue. For example, if you are at a gas station, and notice frustration at the cost of fuel from the person pumping gas next to you, it might be an opportuni-ty to throw out one or two facts about energy—a personal story would be even better. In this venue, there isn't enough time to start a dissertation on global trade agreements, and it would be awkward, irrelevant, and a waste of time to broach the topic of immigration, for example. Or while you and other parents are waiting for the children to get out of school, there might be an opportunity to make them aware about the recent budget controversies going on at the school district. In contrast, showing up at a group's pro-test unaccompanied to counter their message is not a good time to voice your opinion; it not only would not be heard, you might be attacked verbally or physically. Neither would

it be productive to assail a neighbor who owns a gun, for example, and berate him about violent crimes committed using guns.

Zones of Awareness and iden-tifying opportunities for community engagement are two tactics to prac-tice in order to face the public successfully and evolve as a Citizen Ninja. Through experience, I learned that what transforms ordinary citizens into powerful and effec-tive Citizen Ninjas is the willingness and the discipline to practice the Citizen Ninja way on a *daily* basis. We must be willing to operate in the assess zone mind-set so that we can actively be seeking and identifying opportunities.

15

Pegging

Political discourse with strangers is unpredictable. When speaking with friends, families, and neighbors, it can be detrimental to personal relationships if we don't approach conversations with tact. Before developing the Citizen Ninja way, I felt stifled when speaking about politics in small groups of friends or with family because I prioritized the relationship over the issues. Conversing with my father or brother, for example, was a bit like walking on eggshells. I knew which topics provoked them and on which ones we disagreed, but I had no sense of how to work around it.

Fortunately, our robust debates have never defined my relationship with my family, but I felt frustrated that more often than not, we avoided talking about controversial issues. I imagine that most of us would rather withhold information and get along than get into an uncomfortable discussion or, worse, an irreconcilable argument with a relative or a friend. The solution to this problem is *pegging*.

Staging Effective Discourse

Pegging is a tactic Citizen Ninjas use to discern audience's knowledge and bias on a topic we want to talk about. For example, when public speaker Citizen Ninja Nancy concludes her lectures, there is generally a Q & A period. To provide the best answer possible, she quickly discerns a person's level of knowledge on the topic by listening to the question while asking herself: Based on the type and content of the question, is this person *informed, uninformed, misinformed,* or *partisan?* If Nancy is talking about civic engagement, for example, a member of the audience might ask her the steps to delivering a public comment to City Council. This basic question tells Nancy that person is *uninformed* and needs basic information.

Alternatively an audience member might indicate that he has experience with writing a blog but would like more specifics on how to reach a more targeted audience. Using the pegging technique, Nancy determines that he is relatively *informed,* because he is already reaching a general audience through his blog. Because he has some basic knowledge, she gives a more in-depth answer. This is pegging—discerning a person's level of knowledge on a topic and interfacing with them at that level. When Citizen Ninjas pursue municipal activities or engage in political discourse, we want to peg whom we are interfacing with to better determine the approach to use. Pegging someone right off the bat saves time, energy, and discomfort, and sets the stage for productive and effective discourse.

Informed People

Pegging people as *informed* means you've determined they have knowledge about the topic being discussed and generally share a similar viewpoint. These people are easy to talk to because you don't have to be guarded. You can relax, and as you exchange information, you deepen your knowledge and have an opportunity to bounce thoughts and ideas around without feeling defensive. When pegging informed people you know you can speak to them directly without need for subtlety.

For example, Citizen Ninja Ollie enjoys going to a monthly men's prayer group because it's an opportunity for him to socialize with like-minded gentlemen. While they share the same values, each person brings a unique viewpoint which stimulates their thinking. Citizen Ninjas can have more detailed and in-depth conversations with informed people as opposed to persons pegged as *uninformed.*

Uninformed People

Uninformed people are those who know a little about the topic of conversation but would like to know more. When Citizen Ninjas speak to uninformed people, we share information gradually. The uninformed can become overwhelmed when we download too much data all at once. They need time to digest the facts and concepts being discussed.

Consider Citizen Ninja April's approach while recruiting new members to her advocacy group, Citizens for Environmental Justice. April and her colleagues have in-depth knowledge about how politics and back-room deals are negatively impacting the poorest neighborhoods in their city. However, when April approaches someone who is interested in joining her advocacy group, she pegs them first to assess their biases and level of knowledge. When the person is uninformed, April doesn't dive into all the politics immediately, flooding them with information. Instead she starts off by introducing the person to the group, invites him or her to one of their events, and shares the group's fundamental mission and goals. This gradual approach is less overwhelming. When you peg uninformed persons, speak to them openly, be patient and disseminate information bit by bit. We make answers to their questions simple and provide only basic information.

Misinformed People

Misinformed people are those who believe they are informed but are actually misguided on their facts. When Citizen Ninjas peg misinformed persons, we answer strictly with facts to support our argument and provide sources they recognize and trust. For example, while sharing information to a group on citizens' rights to not have to identify themselves when addressing a governing body, an audience member challenged Citizen Ninja Ly, declaring she was incorrect. The challenger claimed he has always been required to state his name when addressing his local school board. Without telling him he was mistaken, Ly explained the facts and guided his knowledge. If Ly had not pegged him as misinformed, her response might have come off as defensive and rude. She might have responded like this: "I'm sorry, but you are mistaken. Look it up. Section Four of the *Brown Act*. It's right there in black and white!"

Citizen Ninjas can expect two different types of responses from misinformed people. The first response is gratitude for being set straight on the facts. They will typically say something like: "Wow! Thank you so much for telling me that. I had no idea! I'll do more research." When they realize they were misinformed and are willing to research more facts, they can be moved to the uninformed category. At this point, they can be educated more directly as long as you are mindful not to overwhelm them with too much information.

The second type of response is defensive, especially when the misinformed are presented with facts that they regard as wrong or in conflict with their beliefs. When you try to educate misinformed persons directly, they can become angry, aloof, or distant. If you persist in educating them, quite often they will walk away, end communication, or use unfounded arguments to shut down the discussion. When you discern this type of person, educate them indirectly.

Inform Indirectly

Educating indirectly means backing off and approaching the misinformed person more subtly. By persisting in righteousness, you can appear domineering, as a 'know-it-all' and arrogant. This doesn't work in your favor and doesn't encourage civil discourse. When misinformed people realizes they are being confronted with new information, they feel exposed and vulnerable. It takes time to process new information, so Citizen Ninjas leave the conversation with one or two facts from sources that the misinformed person trusts.

We all have favorite sources, and misinformed people are no different. For example, liberals tend not to trust facts generated by conservative think tanks, just as conservatives tend to scorn facts pulled from liberal news journals. The irony is that facts are facts regardless of the source. The dynamic you have to work around is prejudice and partiality. When using sources in support of your argument the misinformed person respects, you neutralize the situation and can get back on message.

In Citizen Ninja Ly's case, she can respond to the doubting audience member by saying: "The great news for citizens is that Section Four of the *Brown Act* states that we do not have to share our name or address when we speak to a Council or Board!" Another indirect approach when pegging a misinformed person at a social gathering, for example, is to continue the discussion with an informed person in the vicinity so the misinformed person hears your comments without being confronted directly.

Another indirect tactic is for another informed person to chime in to "help" by supporting you with similar facts. As a Citizen Ninja, however, be cautious with this option. Your goal is to promote civil discourse in these situations, not conflict and discord. By teaming up with others, misinformed persons might feel attacked or 'ganged up on.' Educating misinformed persons indirectly is a non-confrontational approach to inform the misinformed person.

Partisan People

Partisan people are those who have a different opinion from yours. Because it is challenging to engage with partisan people, Citizen Ninjas deploy the power of self-restraint. Many Citizen Ninjas enjoy speaking with partisans, especially when they know the facts and can keep their cool. Citizen Ninjas find it helpful to hear facts, thoughts, and opinions from people who don't share their ideologies. When, however, you discern that partisan persons cannot regulate their emotions and are likely to become belligerent, switch topics or leave the conversation. Partisan people who resort to bullying those with differing views are not engaging in civil discourse; they are endeavoring to discredit you.

Consider my Citizen Ninja experience. I was invited to speak to a church group for thirty minutes about the benefits of local control of education standards. It quickly became clear that a partisan bully was in attendance. He interrupted my presentation with an obnoxious comment. He was sitting directly in the center of the audience. Apparently he wanted me to see him. He interrupted me five times during my thirty minute presentation. Each time he interrupted, I allowed him to speak but I did not respond. Had I done so, I would have given him control of the conversation. I sensed the audience was getting agitated. He disagreed with my premise that schools perform better when standards, curriculum, and spending decisions are made at the state and local levels in lieu of the federal level. But instead of waiting for the Q&A portion of the evening to challenge my premise thoughtfully and intelligently, he seemed to be trying to discredit me.

During the Q&A, he finally said: "Looking around this room, I can see that I'm probably the most intelligent person here. There is *nothing* you've said tonight that would convince me to believe you. Facts aren't everything."

A man in the back of the room stood up and disagreeing passionately shared his story in support of my thesis. When the speaker finished, a woman stood up, saying supportive comments. After her, another person shared, and then another, and another. These testimonials went on for twenty minutes! I didn't speak during their declarations. It was an amazing and rare moment to witness. The audience had literally circled their wagons around me to ward off the partisan bully. He left several minutes later. The beauty was that even though the partisan bully had insulted the audience members, they never returned the insult and instead addressed him indirectly; there was never a direct attack on him. Instead they spoke the truth of their experience.

As people in the audience were leaving, several commented on how grateful they were that I had managed the evening so well. I told them they should feel good because they had not only found the courage to speak but had inspired all with their personal stories. Not everyone will like what you present or agree with your view. It's okay to have differing opinions. What is not okay is a partisan bully who disrupts the discourse.

Citizen Ninjas who peg partisan persons generally avoid political discourse with bullies, especially when they seem to be trying to shut down the conversation. When Citizen Ninjas find themselves in a confrontation with partisan bullies, the best approach is to speak to them respectfully, truthfully, and most importantly, to remain in control. Mirroring antagonism elevates the tension. When dealt with calmly, partisan bullies who try to take us down fail, because their own bad behavior exposes them as the aggressors.

Consider Citizen Ninja Joel, the leader of a grassroots organization devoted to defeating terrorism. Radical anti-Israeli groups were issued a permit to demonstrate in support of Palestinians. Restraining his immediate angry reaction, Joel paused and, thinking like a Citizen Ninja, he thought, "This calls for a response, not a reaction."

Joel, having pegged the protestors as partisans, discussed with members of his organization ways to respond. They determined meeting head to head with the protestors would not foster civil dialogue. It was important to Joel's group they be portrayed as peaceful counter-protestors rather than antagonistic ones. Working with a local synagogue, Joel developed a powerful plan to counter the protest with a small group that would peacefully hold up Israeli flags. There would be no chanting and no protest signs—just a silent stand-off. Joel knew he couldn't control how the protestors would react to their peaceful counter-protest, but he hoped it might foster constructive dialogue between the two groups. Videographers were stationed around the group to capture any activity that might unfold...and unfold it did.

Four hundred protestors marched, loudly chanting hateful slogans, while Joel and his Citizen Ninjas stood across the street silently holding their flags high. The flags were irresistible to the angry protestors and provoked them to launch hate-filled epithets. The small band of Citizen Ninjas remained calm and peaceful, which further enraged the protestors. The protest became chaotic when suddenly a smaller mob charged the peaceful counter-protestors. Joel and his band of Citizen Ninjas retreated to safety. Later, on the local news, the reporter showed video footage of Joel's peaceful band being accosted by aggressive anti-Israeli protestors, which unfortunately, exposed them as an angry and belligerent mob unwilling to be civil.

Citizen Ninjas know that partisan bullies generally have little interest in civil discourse, so avoid them when possible. When they can't be avoided, Citizen Ninja's calmly expose the bullying behavior rather than becoming bullies.

Pegging people as informed, uninformed, misinformed, or partisan is an essential component of the Citizen Ninja way for engaging in political discourse. It develops discernment skills and promotes more productive and effective discourse. Armed with your four Citizen Ninja powers, zones of awareness, and pegging, you are now ready to learn how to ask a question.

16

Ask Questions

Now that you are armed with the four Citizen Ninja powers, you know how to operate in well-defined zones of awareness, how to identify opportunities, and understand how to peg your audience—it's time to speak!

Citizen Ninjas who identify a worthwhile opportunity for engagement, start by *asking questions.* Imagine standing in the 8:00 a.m. Motor Vehicles Department queue waiting for the doors to open at 9:00 a.m. Because you're a Citizen Ninja, you're listening and assessing whether or not the people on either side of you might be willing to have a conversation. With a smile and asking a simple question most people drop their guard and will chat with you.

Rather than making a statement, use a question to initiate a chat. Questions prompt people to respond. Neutral questions like: "What brings you to the DMV today?" might yield discussions on government pensions or immigration. "Crazy weather we're having this fall. What do you think we should expect this winter?" is more likely to produce a conversation about climate change or cost of energy. One question leads to another and in no time at all, you're engaging in a dialogue. Citizen Ninjas listen for cues to help assess other's viewpoints and then peg their knowledge level. The goal is to engage people in political discourse and share ideas. Starting with a question draws people out.

Steps to Success

Citizen Ninjas use the following steps to initiate discussion. First, pick a topic you're knowledgeable about and comfortable with. Asking a question is the best way to introduce a topic, gauge interest, and expose someone's opinion. For example, let's say you happen to bump into a neighbor while in line at the post office. The topic is water conservation, because you noticed that despite Texas being in a 4-year drought, the post office is skirted by a green lawn. To start the topic of conversation, ask a question, such as, "What do you think about all this green grass on public property while we are struggling through a drought?"

Be assertive and inject a secondary topic; government accountability, such as, "What do you think about all this green grass on public property when City Hall has been pressuring us to conserve water during a drought?"

Listen as the person responds. There is a tendency to not listen attentively to the person's reply because you may be formulating your follow-up comment. Citizen Ninjas resist this impulse; instead, pause and listen carefully. When the person replies, peg him or her to discern the person's degree of knowledge on the topic.

A response by an *informed person* might be: "I think it's totally irresponsible and unfair to those of us who are sacrificing our own water usage." A response by an *uninformed person* might be: "I didn't notice." And a response by a *misinformed person* might be: "The drought is short-term and city property should look good."

How to Educate

Depending on the answer, you may choose to educate the person directly or indirectly. When you discern the person is informed, you might ask: "The city should be a role model for water conservation if they expect the community to sacrifice their own water usage. Would you be willing to speak up at the next council meeting?"

Alternatively, if you peg the person as uninformed or misinformed, you can take a moderate approach and respond indirectly. For example you might ask, "I have noticed that there are other cities that are leading the charge on water conservation by swapping lawns for drought tolerant plants. It really looks beautiful! Perhaps the city could benefit from us suggesting alternative landscaping ideas. Would you be willing to call city hall?"

Talking with an uninformed or misformed person takes speaking with more tact. You may ask a follow up question as another way to educate indirectly. Or you may end the conversation by not asking a follow-up question. Finally, if a conversation becomes intense, threatening, or angry is increasing, you can disengage politely.

Citizen Ninjas sometimes use humor to defuse heated conversations by injecting levity. Resist sarcasm as it is a passive/aggressive approach that can disrupt your efforts to engage in civil discourse. Remember that *you* guide the conversation. When you feel uncomfortable, you can disengage at any time. The choice is yours.

Citizen Ninja Carla's approach to a bullying parent on her son's new basketball team provides an example of how to flip an uncomfortable situation you can't avoid into a tolerable one. Carla didn't know the parents on the team yet and the first time she attended practice she neglected to remove her name tag following a political meeting. Seeing it, one of the parents made a snarky comment about her political affiliation. Carla could have ignored him but wanted to feel at ease in the stands.

She stepped back from her agitation and decided to use the Citizen Ninja way to neutralize this guy's jibes. At the next practice she sat beside him and shared her interest in knowing his political views and how he had formed them. Carla asked, "Hey Dan, you obviously know that I'm a Republican. I was wondering which political ideology you align with? How did you form your opinions about that?" Carla listened and asked questions to draw him out, which communicated to Dan that Carla had a genuine interest in his point of view. By asking a question, Carla shifted the focus away from having to defend herself to Dan, who was willing to share his opinions and experiences. Her decision to engage positively with Dan prompted many future civil political discussions in the stands. Sometimes they agreed and often they did not, but both Carla and Dan agreed to be tolerant of each other's differences.

Know the Facts

When speaking before a larger group, such as at a conference, an adult education course, or a public meeting, make sure to know the facts before engaging. Research the topic ahead of time so you are prepared with facts and sources.

When armed with facts, you can challenge false claims, and misleading or omitted information made by the speaker. Speakers (no matter who they are) generally have strong beliefs. Perhaps they are experts in their field and have compelling opinions based on facts. Audience members may or may not agree with the speaker.

That is fine, but realize most people view the speaker as an authority on the subject and are in attendance because they want information from such an expert. The last thing they want is to have the speaker's presentation interrupted.

Wait until the Q&A portion of the presentation to ask a question or make a statement. Challenge speakers when they make false claims, share misleading information, or omit important data, and avoid arguing over ideology. If you want to address a partisan issue, reach out to the speaker afterwards. People who haven't learned the Citizen Ninja way make the mistake of being argumentative during a presentation, becoming the 'bad guy' in the eyes of the public. Unrestrained outbursts make them vulnerable to verbal attacks and hurt their credibility. The goal is not to change the mind of the speaker but to educate.

Speak to the Group

Speaking to groups is an opportunity to educate a larger public around you so they might become more knowledgeable. When speaking at a congressional town hall meeting or at a conference/seminar, for example, you have an opportunity to inform the public at large by the type of questions you ask.

Consider Citizen Ninja Serge, who formulated a question while attending a 100% Clean Energy Forum that would give the appearance he was in favor of implementing enforceable climate action plans (CAP) and would simultaneously reveal to the audience that city CAPs are voluntary and not mandated by the state. Serge wanted the audience to know this fact and wanted the elected public servants, who had already implemented a voluntary CAP, to reveal how they got consensus from their constituents. Towards this end he asked: "Given that the California Global Warming Solutions

Act is voluntary for cities, how did you implement an enforceable CAP?"

Serge was shocked when a panelist who was, a deputy mayor admitted to working around the public by conducting behind-the-scenes persuasive meetings with City staff, developers, and environmental NGO/NPOs to advance the City's CAP. Serge's question revealed that CAPS are voluntary to the audience, and the deputy mayor's response exposed the unethical tactics used to push the CAP through.

Stay Civil

Consider senior Citizen Ninja Solange. In retirement, she enjoys matriculating in adult education classes to further her education in new subjects. While Solange has found satisfaction with this activity, her professors often deliver incorrect facts to support their personal opinions in order to influence students' thoughts.

Rather than ignore the professors' attempts to impose their agenda on students, Solange used the Citizen Ninja way to engage her professors in a civil manner. Using her tablet or smartphone, she adeptly looked up assertions made by her professors to verify the veracity of their claims. When she discovered that the assertions manipulated the facts, she politely exposed the professor's misleading information—simultaneously educating the other students. For example, during a course on feminism and gender studies, her professor was discussing Margaret Sanger, the founder of the first birth control league in the early 20th Century. Solange respectfully challenged the professor's statement that Sanger's revolutionary approach to solving poverty was motivated primarily by social justice. "Professor, in her book, *The Pivot of Civilization,* Sanger wrote that she was motivated by protecting an elitist class rather than to seek social justice.

As another example, in an indigenous studies class, Solange politely presented new information to the class when her professor scorned the colonialists' impact on the indigenous landscape. "Professor, what do you think of the thesis Charles Mann presents in his book, *1491,* that the indigenous American culture was as agriculturally innovative as their European counterparts, shaping and controlling their environment to suit their needs?" Solange's goal was not undermining the professor but rather to educate the other students by introducing new facts.

Asking a Question along with Zones of Awareness, Identifying Opportunities, and Pegging, are foundational to the Citizen Ninja way. Citizen Ninjas cannot face the public successfully without them. They are the gateway tactics that help transform us from ordinary citizens to powerful and effective Citizen Ninjas!

17

Resource Management

It's empowering to engage in the public square with a strategy, effective tactics, and knowledge. The Citizen Ninja way is a strategy for engagement that gives confidence because the tactics foster a productive approach to civic activism. As Citizen Ninjas, we are on a persistent quest for effective municipal participation and civil political discourse in the public square. We seek an exchange of ideas, robust debate, respect, and tolerance to counter those of today's tactics which promote violence, hatred, prejudice, and bullying. To help with this quest, it is imperative that you be equipped with a battery of factual data that are derived from multiple legitimate sources.

Resource management is a key component to credibility, efficiency, and success. Greater yet is being able to spend more time engaging in politics and government rather than being bogged down by disorganization and hours of inefficient research techniques. Technology offers a way to improve how we collect and manage resources, and helps ordinary citizens transition into powerful Citizen Ninjas. The traditional practices of researching, clipping, filing, storing, and sharing information can be accomplished using a variety of electronic tools.

Source Material

Let's first talk about *source material*. Online news sources and blogs dramatically increase access to information. It's like having a jar of jelly beans at your disposal, like Bertie Botts and Harry Potter. You can eat them all, but how do you know which jelly beans are good? It is the same with the Internet. Credibility is sacred to Citizen Ninjas, so where you acquire information is vital. There are hundreds of Internet sites that exist solely to spread disinformation for the purpose of pitting groups against each other. Disinformation is like a virus. When it is not contained it spreads quickly, provoking people to react emotionally and impulsively.

Before assuming a source is legitimate, Citizen Ninjas consider the following: What are the author's qualifications and credentials, and his or her connections to the subject and organization? What is the author's motivation? Selling a product? Why is the author writing the article? Is there bias? Is the purpose to report objective facts only? Or is the author presenting an opinion? How many references are mentioned? Are the sources authoritative? Have other authors presented similar facts derived from other sources? Vet sources carefully and, before sharing any information, corroborate the story with previously vetted news sources.

Use Personal Stories

Gathering information and knowledge is one thing but knowing what and how to share it is another. Source material should come from a variety of places, but the most compelling source is personal experience. Telling a personal story is a profound way to reach an audience. We are naturally drawn to the human experience. There is no greater truth witnessing and sharing an event. Generally we want to feel empathy for others and in return hope for understanding.

I can impart a multitude of empirical data during a presentation, but it will pale before the power of a personal story. That is because people relate better to the human experience than to data. Stories put facts into context. When you engage in political discourse with someone, consider opening with a personal story. Then support the story with relevant facts.

Facts derived from typical secondary resources like newspapers, reports, or documents are essential, but they pale in comparison to facts obtained from primary sources. A primary source is original evidence or information, or material from witnesses. When you attend a conference, interview a key player, or visit a site, you exponentially elevate the truth of your argument because you were there to experience it. Capturing primary source information and sharing it with others increases credibility and shows others your commitment and thoroughness.

For example, I often speak on land use and property rights, and the lack of coordination happening between Federal agencies like the Environmental Protection Agency (EPA) or regional boards like the California Coastal Commission (CCC), and local County and City jurisdictions. The audience's reception to this news is generally lukewarm until I share stories like the one of an older couple who wanted to subdivide their property into four parcels and were prevented from doing so by the EPA unless they designated a portion of their land as a conservation preserve, or the four sisters who wanted to rebuild a barn that had deteriorated over the years and were denied a permit by the CCC unless they agreed to apportion a segment of their property to a public easement so the public could pass through their property to access the beach. In each situaiton I interviewed the property owners, walked their property with them, and reviewed their material. They were my primary sources.

In both cases, the local County Board of Supervisors or City Council had approved the permits but were then overruled by the EPA and CCC respectively. The older couple's story gets even more shocking. They had witnessed strangers trespassing onto their property while depositing a smattering of unmarked rudimentary animal catch boxes and blowing a bird call whistle that resembled the sound made by the gnatcatcher, a California bird listed as an endangered species. The couple speculated undercover EPA agents were attempting to catch endangered animals in the boxes giving them just cause for the conservation preserve mandate. Stories are evidence and they have a greater impact on us than just slogging through facts.

Secondary Sources

The next best evidence after personal stories and primary source information are secondary sources—research reports, documents, and news and editorial outlets. Secondary sources are useful especially when you have limited funds and time. When I begin researching a topic, I spend hours on the Internet, reading books, articles, and reports. Frankly, it is overwhelming, and I spend a fortune on ink cartridges, paper, folders, and file boxes. My desk is littered with piles of paper, and even though I may have a loose sense of how the resources are organized, it may take me more than 20 minutes to locate the facts I need—that is 18 minutes too long!

A way to work around this waste of time is to use applications that do the research for you and deliver it right into your electronic mailbox. To save hours of research time, I use a service called Google Alerts™, provided for free by

Google™. This powerful tool is like having a private Internet librarian at my disposal. Google Alerts™ is a service that generates search engine results, based on criteria provided by the user, and delivers the results to his or her inbox. After I set up my search parameters using key words, the service does the rest.

Every day I receive a daily digest of relevant news, videos, and blogs in my email box. After quickly scanning the collection of news items, I pick those relevant to my subject to vet. Next I electronically save worthy articles for future reference. Many politicians, candidates for office, government agencies, and non-governmental organizations have Google Alerts™ on themselves so they know when something is written about them. For example, when Citizen Ninja Alicia's daughter won a state pageant title, she set up a Google Alert™ on her daughter so that she would be alerted when a news organization or blog mentioned her daughter. Google Alerts™ are like the proverbial "canary in the coal mine." They alert you to current national and international trends, gossip, and newsflash points before you have time to find the information yourself.

Digital Clips

As you acquire information you want to save, you might use a digital clipping tool that gives the ability to electronically file the information in pre-assigned folders. By adding tags and comments to the file, you facilitate the retrieval of that information for a later date. Since the information is stored using 'cloud' technology, you only need your username and password to access it. This enables you to travel with your entire library. Services and applications like Google Drive™, Microsoft Office™, Evernote™, and Drop Box™ are examples of online tools that can help you to manage resources and to have immediate access using electronic devices such as smartphones and notepads. It is easy to be assertive when you have quick access to information.

In combat, the ninja warrior was equipped with a weapon for every situation—from close quarter melees to long range targets. To face the public successfully, you need to have a collection of facts, data, and information at the ready. It is critical to be organized, and be able to quickly access resources. Citizen Ninjas have trustworthy and credible reputations because we conscientiously manage resources, use pegging, and the power of self-restraint to determine what and how to disseminate information.

18
Make Statements

S tatements from Citizen Ninjas are not haphazard speech; they are strategic and intentional and are delivered using a variety of tools. Citizen Ninjas don't necessarily expect a response when speaking unless we've asked a question. We've learned that after asking a question, we listen to peg the audience to determine a course of action—retreat, ask another question, or respond with a statement.

Effective Statements

Effective statements start with active listening and pegging so you know the person's level of knowledge and if you speak the same language. Typical conversations tend to not be productive when you assume the people you are dialoguing with understand your language; this may not be so. To resolve this problem, listen and adjust to the language of the people you're seeking to connect with.

How would you define economic freedom?

Let's say, for example, that a Citizen Ninja liberal wants to influence an independent voter to join the Democrat party.

Instead of assuming that the target person defines 'economic freedom'—*as a market system in which the government
regulates the economy to level the playing field*—he might ask:
"How do you define economic freedom?" If the answer is: *a
free market system that encourages equal opportunity and high
standard of living,* then he knows their language differs from
his. As a Citizen Ninja, the next statement might be to find
common ground or mutual understanding. "I agree that quality of life and equal opportunity are important. Do you think
it's possible to achieve a fair and level playing field without
government regulations?" Making this statement encourages
continuing the conversation. By contrast, criticizing the target person's definition promises to end productive discourse.
It's difficult to create desirable outcomes when you are not
speaking the same language as your target audience.

Citizen Ninja Tools of Trade

Citizen Ninjas use numerous tools to share a message. Statements can be written, spoken, visual, be one sentence, a
word, or an entire presentation. There are traditional ways
to make a statement like writing a letter to the editor,
delivering a public comment, distributing a press release, or
sending out email blasts. If you have financial resources you
can advertise your statement on radio, TV, billboards, or
mailers, or if you have limited resources, buttons, rallies, flyers, elevator speeches, videos, and T-shirts are cost effective
ways to get your message out. Just as traditional tools have
stood the test of time and continue to be effective, the new
cyber technology delivers a variety of powerful applications.
Some of my favorites are YouTube™, Facebook™, Twitter™,
LinkedIn™, Power Point™, and blogging. They may require
more technological aptitude to use, but the investment in
learning how to use them is worth it.

Review your strengths. Are you more comfortable speaking, writing, or both? What is your technological aptitude?
Based on your skills and preferences, look at the list of

available tools, and on a sheet of paper list in one column the tools you already use; in another column, list those you are willing to try. It is helpful to start with tools you are comfortable with, then to push yourself and try new methods of communication.

Tools Citizen Ninja Use

Traditional Tools		
Letter to the Editor	Presentation	Billboard
Newsletter	Advertisement	Signage
Public Comment	Buttons/Pins	Flyer
Elevator Speech	Postcard	Letter
Resolutions	Rally	
Press Release	Radio	
Cyber Tools		
Facebook	Twitter	Electronic Tablet
YouTube	Blog	Video
Power Point	Smart Phone	Email
Infographic		

Sharing thoughts out loud is challenging because speech requires preparation, mental agility, and, sometimes, instantaneous critical thinking skills. The more time you spend researching and developing your thoughts, the easier it is to make statements in a public setting. For example, I'm more comfortable with writing, so I started there. Email and Facebook™, were easy since I had a built-in audience of friends, family, and acquaintances. Eventually, I pushed myself to create a blog. From a technical standpoint the process was challenging but with useful DIY resources I was successful. I felt a degree of anxiety the first time I pushed the "publish" button on my blog page but I didn't let that stop me. By generating an article every couple of weeks, it didn't take long before I was reaching an international audience! The more I researched and wrote, the more my opinions developed. This natural evolution of ideas, expressed in the written word, prompted me to feel more comfortable using the spoken word.

Interestingly, my experience with writing has demonstrated that blogging, generating newsletter articles, or writing letters to the editor are often easier to do than shorter statements like an elevator speech, postcard, or public comment. An elevator speech is a 20-60 second summary statement that defines a project or an association's mission, purpose, and value. When our non-profit board of directors and advisors collaborated to create our own elevator speech, it took about three hours to massage the who, what, and why of our organization into a 60 second blurb. Shorter statements require dumping extraneous matter in order to formulate a precise message.

Keep it Short

People are busy, so keep it concise! A well-crafted summary statement can get your foot in the door whether you are lobbying at the State Capitol, introducing a new project to potential donors, or sharing your vision for a new fundraising campaign. Or, instead of emailing protracted text to advertise an upcoming event, you might write short statements or ask questions to draw people's attention. For example, when I advertise an upcoming *How to Become a Citizen Ninja* workshop, I ask three quick questions on the flyer to grab attention, pique interest, and identify who would benefit from attending the workshop. "Do you worry about being marginalized by expressing your opinion in public? Have you been bullied in a public forum or town hall meeting? Do you wonder if civil discourse is even possible?"

INFOGRAPHICS

Capture the essence of your message without being bogged down by blocks of letters

WHY YOU NEED THEM

20%
is all we remember after reading text

90%
of info relayed to the brain is visual

200%
more images over texts are liked on social media

12%
Avg boost in traffic after publishing an infographic

Who Reads Infographics?

TEXT
IMAGES

85% more likely to read

Everyone   Would Rather Read   Infographics

Crowds Are Opportunities

Citizen Ninjas never let a crowd go to waste. Whenever there is a gathering of people, be ready and armed with hand-outs. Hand-outs or flyers are a great way to communicate directly with the public and reach low information voters, for example. I know of Citizen Ninjas who will show up at town fairs, parades, festivals, and farmers' markets and walk up and down the street handing out flyers and

Citizen Ninjas never let a crowd go to waste.

wearing t-shirts or buttons to advertise their cause. This activity is fruitful because it prompts people to stop and chat about

the information being disseminated. Traditional hand-outs, however, are not as effective as *infographics*.

Infographics are a dynamic and pithy way to communicate a message without saturating the page with too many words. Because they are graphically rich, they often communicate the message via photos, illustrations, graphs, and charts, eliminating the practice of using sentences and

paragraphs. At a glance the reader can capture the essence of the message without getting bogged down by blocks of letters. Such infographics whet the readers' appetite and offer links to websites for more information. There are a myriad of infographic websites that offer basic templates free to help you get started.

Images Move Us

Each tool has its purpose and should be selected appropriately. Often, the power of images can have a greater impact on people's emotions than do words, and therefore the use of photography and video should be considered. We can read about human trafficking all day long and develop a distaste for it, but there is nothing like a video segment or a photograph of a drugged-out 15-year-old girl to drive home the message that human trafficking is wrong and needs action. Depending on the issue, visual communication can speed things along, prompting the audience to respond.

Citizen Ninjas who prefer visual statements have a YouTube™, channel to post and report videos or repost. After a video is posted, a shorter web address called a "tinyURL" is generated to make sharing easier on Facebook™, and Twitter™, and elsewhere. Recorded material is primary source information and tells the story as it happened. Be wary of sharing videos you didn't create. Sometimes unethical people cut out segments of a politician's speech, for example, so the politician's remarks seem extreme, uninformed, or stupid. When a video has been edited, always find and watch the full version to get the context for the edit.

Use the Power of Video

Video keeps public servants honest and transparent. Consider Citizen Ninja Steve, who lives in a small rural community. The first time he attended a City Council meeting, he was appalled by how unprofessional the City Council looked and how informally they communicated with one another. Their countenance did not match their serious role as governors of his City. At the next meeting, Steve recorded the proceedings of the next meeting and posted it on You-Tube™, and emailed the video with his friends, family, and acquaintances.

After recording and posting five City Council meetings, Steve noticed that all five City Council people had spiffed up and were now wearing suits and button down shirts! Their interactions were less familiar and more aligned with proper business conduct. By exposing their conduct on You-Tube™, i.e. to the public, Steve influenced the Council to be more conscientious about their behavior and appearance.

As a Citizen Ninja, you routinely seek opportunities to educate those around you. Choose appropriate language. For example, when composing a public comment it is natural to think that the sole audience is the City Council. The audience is broader than that, however, including the public sitting behind you along with those watching the live feed from home, for example.

Frequently, members of the public, like Citizen Ninja Steve, use a smartphone to record meeting and post clips from it online. This is a huge opportunity to extend your reach. All the more reason that your statements are written thoughtfully and spoken clearly. When making statements on Facebook™, for example, you have the potential to reach a vast network of followers. You might set up group forums open to the public, or consider using Facebook™ as an electronic billboard to share articles, photos, and videos for your Facebook™ friends to view.

Stick to the Facts

When posting a statement on Facebook™, it is more effective when your message is supported by facts. Facebook™ and other social media are a kind of "water cooler" hangout where conversations take place. Sometimes, unfortunately the anonymity fosters juvenile and un-civil discourse.

Consider Citizen Ninja Maurice, whose Facebook 'friend,' Imani, made a strong personal statement on her page about abortion within the black community without any supporting facts. Maurice was annoyed but resisted the urge to lash out at her irresponsible statement. Imani's Facebook™ friends were polarized on this issue, many resorted to name calling. Some supported Imani's position that the abortion industry was helping black women stem the tide of poverty; others like Maurice believed that abortion clinics were disproportionally hurting black families by setting up their clinics in predominantly black neighborhoods. Instead of adding to the list of reciprocal insults, Maurice changed the tone of the thread by asking a series of questions to uncover the basis for Imani's statement. When they establish some shared basic principles, Maurice turned the conversation from name-calling into a meaningful discussion of the issue based on facts and real examples.

Making productive and effective statements requires Citizen Ninjas to be active listeners to peg the audience to determine people's level of knowledge on the topic and their language. Be mindful of the audience around you. Identify your target audience. Communicate with statements using a variety of traditional and cyber tools. Be careful the statements themselves are succinct.

19

The Power of Words

To Citizen Ninjas, words are a mighty tool for communication. Words are powerful, whether used for ill or good, and can be fraught with pitfalls that have the potential to throw us off course. Words pierce like a warrior sword so when Citizen Ninjas speak, we choose words to edify not to wound, slander, corrupt, or deceive.

Citizen Ninjas understand there are people (strange or familiar), organizations, and elected public servants and staff who use words to corrupt and deceive, and they do so in part to influence public opinion. They wrap their words in warm and fuzzy terms to gain consent or they change the definition of words to persuade the public to agree with their agenda. Attempts to manipulate language are factors we cannot control, but we should be wary of them all the same. What Citizen Ninjas can control is how we manage manipulated language. To inject clarity and truth into our discourse, listen critically to the words you hear to glean the intent behind the language, and as you learned in the last chapter, be selective with the words you speak and write to maximize communication.

Believe me when I say...

Warm and Fuzzy Language

Advertising agencies, government entities, media, entertainment, and public relations companies carefully choose language to persuade, influence, build consensus and ensure compliance of an unsuspecting public. Their manipulated language influences the way we think about things, events, culture, people, and ideas.

Words move people to action.

Citizen Ninjas listen to understand, and interpret the subtle language that appears in the guise of warm and fuzzy terms meant to disarm and sway public opinion toward a specific and calculated desired outcome. A simple example of warm and fuzzy is to highlight the two distinct feelings we get from watching Coors Lite™ and Anheuser-Busch™ commercials. Coors Lite™ commercials picture people in frozen arctic scenes in order to relay the message of cold and fresh.

Anheuser-Bush™ commercials portray horses and puppies in a cold environment caring for and helping each other—conveying a warm and fuzzy message.

Terms such as *gun violence, boots on the ground,* and *shock and awe* are all examples of intentionally crafted language. The term, *gun violence,* for example, makes us think of the gun as being violent when actually it is the person brandishing the gun who is violent. *Boots on the ground* makes us think of high-top combat shoes, not soldiers in combat with limbs blown off, and *shock and awe* are simply emotional reactions, not horrendous physical injuries due to massive bombings.

Soft Language

When confronted with unpleasant and frightening topics like war, terrorism, and aggression, shifting from direct words to soft ones makes us feel better because soft language is more tolerable than sharply spoken truths. Media headlines like *work place violence* and *kinetic military action*

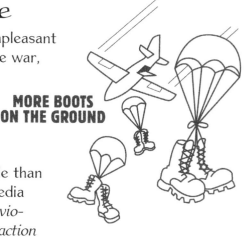

MORE BOOTS ON THE GROUND

alarm people less than when they hear terms like *domestic terrorist attacks* and *acts of war*, which are frightening. Most people react negatively to the words *attack* and *war*, and in contrast gloss over the words *disaster* and *action*, just as *an uncontested arrival* is a lot more palatable than *an invasion*. Soft words may take more effort to say the same thing as with direct words, but they can be deceptive and change the focus of the message. Resist being cajoled by soft language. For example, if you hear media use a term like *overseas contingency operation*, listen critically to the intent of the message—rather than trust the term—know they are actually referring to *global war on terror*.

Words move people to action. When language is direct, people will listen and are more likely to act to either protect or thwart the issue at hand. When language is softened, people are inclined to dismiss it and focus on their personal life. The result of using soft language is a public that is less engaged with the issues. This passivity is because people have not been alarmed, rather than not caring.

> Resist being cajoled by soft language.

Why manipulate the language if the intent is to be direct and truthful, you might wonder. When confronted with manipulative languare in a meeting or a casual conversation, ask for clarity to interpret the language and expose the truth behind the soft words. For example you might ask: "You just used the term *revenue enhancement* when describing the new tax laws. What does that term mean? Is this proposed bill referring to tax increases?" Establishing clarity in the language sets the correct tone for discourse.

What does that term mean?

Direct Language

In the world of land use, urban planning, and development, an entirely new vocabulary has been drafted to encourage consensus by the public when it comes to changes in local or regional general plan updates. When Citizen Ninja Arlo attended his city's Planning Commission meetings and heard warm and fuzzy terms like *smart growth, sustainable development,* and *resilient cities,* he asked the Board to clarify them. Arlo is not an urban planning expert, so it was difficult to gauge what they meant by these terms. By requesting clarification, Arlo pressed the Board to reveal to the public at large the intent behind the soft language before proceeding. Urban planning terms like *ecomobility* and *cool cities* evoke a good feeling and a positive attitude about whatever "it" is, but Citizen Ninjas ask to know what these terms mean in direct language.

Ask for Clarity

It's easy to get thrown off course when trusting the feelings that are conjured by warm and fuzzy terms. For example, when hearing the term *smart growth,* we contrast the adjective smart with the word stupid. Naturally, we want to be smart about how we design our community. Smart growth sounds reasonable, and because the term is inherently suggestive we have an immediate attraction to the idea before we know the details. Instead of interpreting the term at face value, do research or ask for clarification to understand the intent behind the warm and fuzzy language. When the term is simplified and understood, your discourse is more direct and candid.

When you ask for clarity and specific definitions at a public workshop for example, you and the audience in the room now understand that the term *road diets* actually specifies lane reduction, and *complete streets* are streets designed for equitable use among cars, bicycles, pedestrians, and transit. When the truth is established you can have proper public deliberation on the merits of such planning strategies. When confronted with warm and fuzzy terms in lieu of simple direct terms, ask the speaker to restate the term using more direct language.

Changing Definitions

A variation on using soft language as a means to influence opinion or make us indifferent is to deliberately and surreptitiously change the assumed common definition of words and substitute a different meaning. For example, the assumed common definition of the word *consensus* is an opinion or position reached by a group as a whole through debate and reasoned judgment. However, Citizen Ninjas are aware that meetings seeking consensus are often micro-managed by experts and facilitators rather than involving discussions by the public to generate ideas and solutions. When public workshop facilitators say "consensus" their adapted definition might be that the decision should be reached by a collaborative process led by experts.

Conflicts can arise when assumed definitions clash with adapted ones because the public is expecting one thing (consensus) and the organizers are offering another (false consensus).

Adapted Language

A common definition of the word *grassroots,* for example, is local community organizing led by the people in collaboration with the state, the market, and non-profits. Challenge public servants who use adapted language—who substitute the following definition for the assumed one: public-private partnerships between the state, the market, and non-profits, in which people can participate. "Sir, your definition of grassroots does not support self-government; in fact it shifts our power to self-govern to governance by influential bureaucratic agencies, corporations, and NPO/NGOs. This is unacceptable. Since the citizens did not initiate this plan, I request that Council form a Citizen's Advisory Committee to review the plan and make recommendations."

Another example of adapted language is the term *fair and equal,* which commonly means we achieve a fair and equal society through reliance on one's own efforts, resources, and abilities rather than those of others. Again, anyone who modifies the term should be confronted to admit their definition is different from the common assumed definition which focuses on self-reliance. "Sir, you are suggesting that a fair and equal society is achieved by reducing material inequalities between individuals or paring our individual success back to the average so that others' results are fair and equitable. Is this correct, and if so, how will our society prosper if we are reliant on others?"

Speak the Same Language

You are probably familiar with the maxim: "When in Rome, do as the Romans do." The Citizen Ninja version is: "When seeking to communicate with someone, use the same language." We discussed the importance of this when you learned how to craft statements, but it is so important to the Citizen Ninja way that the lesson bears repeating.

This Citizen Ninja maxim is a good reference because two people speaking the same language can communicate more successfully than one who speaks Italian and the other Japanese, for example. It is important to recognize, too, that culture is inherently connected to language. Not understanding culture results in a lost-in-translation experience. The same is true when using political language and operating within a particular political culture. You have to understand the vocabulary being used, and to be familiar with the person or group's culture, partiality, or prejudice, when dealing with urban planners, developers, environmentalists, minority groups, and so on.

Because Citizen Ninjas engage people, it benefits us to listen carefully to the person or group speaking in order to assess the language. By listening you discover the political and cultural values and beliefs in play so you can speak accordingly. Becoming proficient at this takes patience, self-restraint, finesse, and discernment. When you listen critically you can create a more open dialogue with a sharing of ideas as opposed to the person who is pushing an agenda, forcing your opinions, or not listening. This ineffective approach often results in antagonism, frustration, bullying, and the use of false arguments or fallacies, which are generally directed at you.

Adapt

To recap: Before engaging someone or a group, know your facts on the issue, ask a question, use pegging to assess the language, and listen to the response. If the person is misinformed or highly partisan, chances are strong that a different language is being used and the person is operating in a different political culture. When you deduce the situation, **adapt**. You might disengage and communicate indirectly—a pegging technique, or continue to engag but use the speaker's preferred language in order to dialogue in a non-threatening manner.

A humorous example that illustrates how people are culturally prejudiced when it comes to words is to share my Citizen Ninja story. My property rights organization board decided to lease a booth at a League of California Cities Conference Expo. The League of California Cities is an association of California city officials, and their conferences are attended by elected public servants, city managers, and the staff who run the various departments, such as Planning, Public Works and Development, Community, and Traffic and Safety Services. The conference expo is an opportunity for vendors to promote goods and services relevant to city management.

Several months earlier, we had compiled a report called *Dimensions of Sustainability: When Considering Smart Growth Planning Policies and Greenhouse Gas Reductions*, which we wanted to hand out to the League members. On the day of the Expo we were surprised by the massive banner across our booth that read: Citizens' Alliance for Property Rights. We were hoping to be stealthier because we knew some people were prejudiced toward the term *property rights* and we didn't want them to shy away from our booth because of words. I created another banner and hung it below the property rights banner. It read: "American Coalition for Sustainable Communities".

Attendees approaching our booth were stymied by the two banners and would stop to inquire. They couldn't figure out the connection between property rights and sustainable communities. The people who were bothered by the words *property rights* revealed their prejudice by sarcastically saying comments such as: "Property rights huh? Where're your guns?" and the people who were put off by the word *sustainable* were appeased by the fact that we were a non-profit property rights organization. At the end of the day we had passed out most of our reports and equally observed that our success in reaching members, no matter their prejudice, had been driven by the power of words.

If a person—strange or familiar, an organization, or public servant is using warm and fuzzy terms or adapted language, Citizen Ninjas stay on course by requesting the use of more direct words or defined words for clarity. Equally, when you identify an opportunity or a person who is using a different language from you, adjust your approach. This saves time, avoids arguing, reduces stress and anxiety, and puts you in control of the conversation.

20
False Arguments

False arguments are rooted in fallacies—false-logic errors in reasoning—crafted to win an argument. Logical fallacies are so common that you may not realize a false argument is being used against you. What is amusing is that kids and parents use false arguments with each other all the time, such as a son protesting, "but dad, everyone has a tattoo!", which is a fallacy called *bandwagon*.

Political leaders, pundits, and media frequently use fallacies to put forth their views when being interviewed on TV news programs. Debate teams quickly learn to avoid using fallacies because the opposing team will neutralize the argument and take the upper hand. Citizen Ninjas also learn to recognize the false-logic argument so they can neutralize or counter them.

Recognize Fallacies

Activists often use false arguments to defeat their opponents. For example, an activist might change the topic to distract from a relevant or important issue, or they may play the role of victim to gain sympathy. False-logic arguments confuse, distract, and disorient an opponent.

Sharpshooters

Legend has it that in the Wild West a certain marksman painted bull's-eye targets around his bullet holes to make it appear they were really good shots. To refute your views, opponents using the sharpshooting fallacy cherry-pick a data cluster to support their argument. Sharpshooting is frequently used by politicians, special interest groups, and NPO/NGOs to advance an agenda.

Fact checking is the weapon for neutralizing sharpshooting. Verify the sharpshooter's claims. Locate and review quoted reports or surveys. Pay attention! Usually the cherry-picked data is accurate, but there may be other statistics in the report that supports a different claim.

Ad-Hominem

Ad-Hominem is an attack directed at the person rather than their position on an issue being discussed. Ad-hominem attacks can take the form of directly attacking someone's character, or more subtly by casing doubt on the person's character to discredit their argument. For example, after Maria Camila spoke articulately about the benefits of parenting, Juan asked the group why they should listen to what a single mother on probation thinks about parenting.

Ad-hominem attacks squash speech and robust debates. For example, instead of trying to win a difficult argument that climate change is not man-caused, a bully can shut down discussion by calling the speaker a "flat-earther" or "climate change denier". As another example, it's easier to call someone a "racist" than to engage in a discussion of divergent opinions.

You can neutralize an ad-hominem attack by calling a spade a spade: "Your argument is an ad-hominem attack that has nothing to do with what we're discussing. Let's find something we can agree on and go from there."

Margaret Thatcher, the former British Prime Minister, said this about ad-hominem attacks: "I always cheer up immensely if an attack is particularly wounding because I think, well, if they attack one personally, it means they have not a single political argument left."

Bandwagon

The bandwagon fallacy is a claim that because many people do something it is a valid action you should follow also. The flaw in this argument is that the popularity of an idea has no bearing on its validity. The demand to jump on the band-wagon drives peer-pressure. It can compel someone to join a cause because it's trendy, or to pressure one to conform to avoid being disenfranchised by the group.

For example, Tasha favored a homosexual candidate because of his stance on pension reforms, but her friends voted for the opposing candidate as a protest vote against a homosexual candidate. Caving in to her friends pressure, Tasha voted against the candidate she silently supported.

The bandwagon fallacy can be neutralized by calling it out: "You all are getting on an emotional bandwagon with this candidate. Rather than focus on his sexual preferences, take a look at his record in comparison to his opponent's. He is clearly the better choice."

Red Herring

Red herring is a fallacy in which an irrelevant topic is presented to divert attention from the actual issue. The basic idea is to "win" an argument by leading attention away from the argument and to another topic. A red herring is also known as a smoke screen.

For example, when former State Assemblyman Chavez, was running for City Mayor, he was questioned by a constituent about his voting record on gun control. Chavez responded: "I'm an open minded individual. What we should really be focusing on is quality education for our children. They are the future of our country." With this Chavez redirected the topic to education to avoid talking about his voting record on gun control.

Here again, the red herring tactic can be neutralized by calling attention to it and restating one's question. For example, when the president of a wind energy company is asked by a reporter to justify the higher energy costs being driven by renewable energy production, he says, "Well, Nancy, that's a great point. Our wind turbines are state of the art and have an excellent maintenance track record. Our energy production is having a positive impact on the environment." Nancy countered this fallacy by saying: "Sir, glad to hear wind turbines are having a positive impact on the environment and your maintenance track record on them is satisfactory. However, you did not answer my question about higher energy costs."

Straw Man

The straw man fallacy misrepresents an argument to make it easier to attack. The trick is to present a counterfeit position that manipulates you into arguing against the straw man rather than your actual position.

For example, after Njere said he wanted Congress to appropriate more funds to the Department of Health for social programs, Leon said he was surprised Njere so hated America that he would leave it defenseless by diverting funds away from the military. Being naive, Njere replied by insisting he loves America.

Be alert for the straw man tactic and don't be led astray. Instead counter this fallacy by saying: "You've just thrown down a straw man, Leon. Our discussion has nothing to do with whether or not I love America."

Appeal to Emotion

Appealing to emotion is meant to elicit an emotional re-sponse to obscure points of an argument. Appeals to fear, envy, hatred, pity, and pride are distractions and, appeals to someone's values can tug powerfully even with those who are wary of these types of false-logic arguments. For example, a city manager might appeal to the city council's pride and say: "You are all so smart and care about the community so much, I'm sure you'll want to get behind this plan." A community organizer seeking to raise funds for an envi-ronmental justice non-profit might appeal to the community's sympathy and say: "If you don't donate what you can today, childhood asthma will increase exponentially."

Fear mongering, for example, is a tactic frequently used by politicians, media, and political activists because people overwhelmingly respond to it. Instead of examining the facts and questioning the merits behind the fear-provoking claim, people are swayed by their emotions.

Often voters choose to not vote for a candidate for fear he will lead them to financial ruin or lead the country to war. Voters rely on what their individual political parties tell them to fear instead of judging each candidate on his track record. Neutralize this fallacy by providing facts, log-ic, and clarity on the point of the argument.

Consider 61-year old Citizen Ninja Charlie who, like many seniors, was concerned about the country's debt lev-el; especially the long-term consequences for his kids and grandkids. At a candidate forum in his retirement complex, a politician cautions the voters about electing his opponent who supports eliminating social security to lower the debt. In that moment, Charlie's fears resonate and his emotions teeter-totter by the politician's appeal to emotion. The politician seemed to be capitalizing on the retirees' fears of retirement security and the consequences of long-term debt. During Q & A, Charlie addressed both candidates: "Instead of fear mongering and appealing to our concerns about social security and the rising debt, perhaps you could each share your plans for creating policy that would both protect social security for retirees and lower the debt."

Charlie's statement neutralized the politician's appeal to emotion fallacy by requesting he focus on solutions instead of people's fears on the issue.

Fallacies on Social Media

Facebook[MT], Twitter[MT] and Linked-In[MT] are widely used platforms upon which people make statements abou issues. It's fascinating how many discussions go awry when someone posts a false argument. Sidetracked by the error in reasoning, people post wildly and the original argument is forgotten. This also happens in the comment sections following web articles and blog posts.

Post and Pushback

Following is a typical Facebook thread among people who disagree with one another. The difference with this conversation is that someone addressed the false arguments. The initial post was a reaction to a Republican presidential candidate who said he would consider a 20-week abortion ban including in cases of rape and incest.

The post read: "I cannot even begin to fathom how one single woman in this country would ever/could ever EVEN CONSIDER voting Republican. These men are just cretins from the Paleolithic Age!!!!!!!" To which another person remarked: "I concur!"

The next response was: "That is a ridiculous statement. I am a Republican and don't appreciate your ad-hominem attacks. Present a logical argument so that we can have civil discourse about this. Protecting innocent babies is not Paleolithic, it's compassionate."

Following up another contributor used the straw man fallacy: "By all means please feel free to adopt, nurture, put these babies through school, etc., etc., etc. Aren't you tired of flogging your medieval values, on and on?"

The final retort came from the person addressing the fallacies. "First of all, I was addressing the Ad-Hominem attacks that were made; I made no mention of being offended by her opinion. Second, why are you introducing medieval religious values into this discussion? And finally, are you willing to have civil discourse about this? Your anger is palpable."

Because many people do not recognize fallacies, they fall prey to them and are led astray, ending up feeling angry, frustrated, or hurt. Citizen Ninjas, on the other hand, are aware of people who use fallacies to undermine their arguments and neutralize the fallacy to get back on message. The Citizen Ninja way is to publically expose the false-logic argument in order to focus on the original argument.

The greatest victory is that which requires no battle.

SUN TZU
6th c. BC Chinese General
and Military Strategist

21

Citizen Ninja Rules

Deploying bully tactics to achieve change or garner attention is not as desirable as being tactically assertive. Bully tactics are intended to intimidate political opponents to force them into compliance to the detriment of the deliberative process. Bullies condone tactics that promote violence, hatred, prejudice and they use verbal and psychological force to discourage, marginalize, discredit, and shut down the public.

Citizen Ninjas on the other hand, use the Citizen Ninja way and a set of rules that encourage the purposeful exchange of ideas, robust debate, and respectful and tolerant interactions in the public square.

The Architect of Activism

Saul Alinsky's *Rules for Radicals,* is a guide for community workers to organize disenfranchised low-income communities, or what he called the "Have-Nots." Alinsky encouraged activists to gain social, economic, and political equality by challenging agencies serving the Have-Nots, claiming they intentionally promoted inequality.

Alinsky emphasized the importance of grassroots activism to bring social change by standing up to entrenched power and references 19th century French political thinker and historian Alexis de Tocqueville's caution that only an enlightened and civically engaged citizenry can protect freedom from an overbearing federal government.

While Alinsky's intent to organize the disenfranchised against the wealthy and the political elite—the Haves—may have been needed in a free society, his revolutionary tactics are destructive to America's political process and civil debate. Alinsky rules use radical tactics—bullying—meant to force changes while discouraging the rational public deliberation that Citizen Ninjas consider so important.

Twelve Alinsky Rules

Alinsky set forth twelve rules that are used relentlessly by politicians, pundits, media, and civil society (NPO/NGOs) to derail and marginalize people. Several of the rules use effective but harsh tactics such as the use of ridicule "to force one's opposition into concessions", focusing on "ways to increase [their] insecurity, anxiety and uncertainty", and isolating opponents by cutting off their supporters. Alinsky encourages radical activists to "pick the target, freeze it, personalize it, and polarize it." Other rules suggest tactics that pressure, destabilize, threaten, and push insistently to force violent reactions by the opposition. And finally, when the opposition caves, he instructs his plebes to always have alternative solutions to the issue at hand.

Power goes to two poles. To those who've got the money and those who've got the people.

SAUL ALINSKY
20th c. Architect of
Modern Activism

Most Americans expect their fellow compatriots to operate using a common code of conduct which directs us to act politely, fairly, and kindly. So when bully tactics are deployed, the public is blindsided and shocked. This is why Alinsky's rules are so effective—they break the code of civility.

Neutralize
Bully Tactics

The Alinsky disenfranchised "Have-Nots" are no longer just racial minority groups or the poor, they are also us—individual members of the public being railroaded, deceived, ignored, and bullied by multi-level stakeholders.

Expect to encounter bullies when you step out into the public square. Bully tactics can be neutralized by learning to recognize and side-step them. Recognizing how and when Alinsky's bully tactics are being used against you is the first step to neutralizing their effect. Become an expert on the issues you care about to make it harder for them to target you and if you do become a target, brush it off to diffuse their attempts to marginalize you. Bullies want to antagonize and force emotional reactions. When you don't respond in kind, their negative energy is diffused. Networking with allies helps to build coalitions and forge alliances. Bullies are less likely to go after a group that is organized, knowledgeable and onto their aggressive tactics.

To be effective, bully tactics like Alinsky's rules, depend on an unwitting public that is ignorant, passive, and swayed by appeals to emotion. Citizen Ninjas who run into such maneuvers side-step them or deflect them just like ninja warriors do who anticipate their opponent's next move or if attacked use their opponent's momentum to deliver a decisive blow.

Citizen Ninja Rules

Alinsky's radical tactics were innovative about how to force a reaction from targeted individuals or organizations. Citizen Ninjas can learn to be just as assertive but to maintain integrity and credibility, the Citizen Ninja way adapts Alinsky's rules and presents them to you as Citizen Ninja Rules.

Rule #1 Training Optimizes Success

Citizens who are trained in the Citizen Ninja way are strategic and tactical. If you decide to act in the public square with untrained cohorts, it's in your best interest to teach and guide them in the Citizen Ninja way before engaging.

Laura had asked members of her Tea Party group to attend regional meetings organized by the State's Environmental Quality Department to protest new restrictive rules on private land use. Without training in productive deliberation, they disrupted the process for no gain. The members were caught off guard when another group—a fierce defender of ecology—bullied Laura's colleagues into ad hominem attacks that painted them as uncooperative and unreasonable people. The experience was so unpalatable they abandoned Laura's group. When Laura learned the Citizen Ninja way she understood the value of training people before sending them to engage in the public square.

Rule #2 Effective Activism Inspires Others

This rule speaks to the Citizen Ninja way. Effective activism leads to habitual and enjoyable civic participation. When you are effective, you become a role model for others who want to emulate similar achievements.

When Laura realized her colleagues left the Tea Party group because they had a bad experience at one of the regional Environmental Quality Department meetings, she organized a training session in the Citizen Ninja way so they would become knowledgeable about how to engage productively in the public square. Developing skills to deflect bullying when publically voicing their opinions, Laura's colleagues were enthusiastic about trying again. Deploying effective strategies and tactics cultivated success and it wasn't long before Laura's group attracted new members.

Rule #3 Create Credentials

From the outside, NPO/NGOs seem like they are large organizations, when often only as few as one to five people run them. As we've discussed, it is common practice to forge public private partnerships, excluding the public from sitting at the stakeholder table. Organizing the community into small coalitions can effectively encourage public participation. A cohesive and organized opposition can be powerful and productive.

Greg was frustrated in his individual efforts to address regional transportation gridlock. So he created an organization with himself as Director. Bureaucrats were more receptive to meeting with him when representing the Project for Smart Transportation than when they saw him as a mere citizen. This Citizen Ninja tactic enabled him to build relationships with other stakeholders. Eventually Greg was invited to join a working group tasked by the County Board of Supervisors with creating alternative solutions to traffic gridlock.

Rule #4 Hold Em' Accountable

Hold individuals, organizations, and government agencies accountable to their set rules and standards. If a politician promises to be accessible to the public or an agency is bound by laws of transparency, it's up to us to point the finger and expose their wrong doing.

Citizen Ninja Rachel's local League of Women Voters chapter, which prizes and posts rules for civil discourse during meetings, failed to stick to their own standards when Rachel presented an opposing view. The board admonished her position and refused to allow any further discussion on the topic. Instead of slinking away, Rachel reminded the League they were not upholding the chapter's rules for civil discourse. Then she proceeded to educate the audience around her that multiple views should be tolerated in a non-partisan organization. The members agreed and a discussion ensued.

Rule #5 Avoid Ruts and Stagnation

Government agencies, administrations, and organizations change leadership frequently which alters dynamics and policies. Stay current and relevant. Consistently evaluate your approach and adjust your strategy and tactics when your efforts begin stagnating.

Citizen Ninja Claire and her cohorts spent a year trying to stop the School District from implementing the new Common Core standards. Though they had some success with other initiatives, like educating parents about their rights to opt their children out of the state assessments, they adjusted their strategy the following scholastic year to invigorate their efforts. They asked new members to be the spokespersons so the board of trustees and the superintendent and her staff would be more receptive to new voices. Instead of focusing on the standards, which had now been implemented, they worked on specific areas that would have a direct impact on Common Core—namely budget, technology, and book adoptions.

Rule #6 Pressure Tactics

Regular and persistent contact with public servants keeps the pressure on them to respond to your requests. Typically, regular citizens give up quickly when they do not succeed right away. Many government agencies and organizations actually intentionally frustrate citizens so they will give up. Always follow-up and stick with it.

By adjusting their strategy to avoid stagnation, and recruiting new members to fight Common Core, Citizen Ninja Claire and her cohorts were able to keep pressuring the board of trustees to address their requests. Reinvigorated, they remained persistent, and their tenacity pressured the board and the superintendent to yield to their demands for more transparency and improved communication.

Rule #7 Shift Public Opinion

Directly provoking individuals, groups, or organizations to react violently against a cause in order to garner sympathy is a dangerous tactic. A safer approach is to provoke a response indirectly by instigating a non-violent strategy that flips the perceived victims into the aggressors.

Recall Citizen Ninja Joel's peaceful counter protest: Instead of mounting a loud and aggressive counter protest, Joel and his small band of Citizen Ninjas chose to stand on a sidewalk and silently wave Israeli flags to counter anti-Israeli demonstrators. The flag waving provoked the anti-Israeli group, and without self-restraint, they crossed the street and lashed out at Joel and his colleagues, winning the media and the public to Joel's side.

Rule #8 Propose Solutions

We all know the old adage: "If you're not part of the solution, you're part of the problem." Opposing an idea, plan, or agenda is good civic participation, but the message is more powerful if it is supported with either practical alternatives or facts that debunk the claims made by the opposition.

Citizen Ninja Chauntel knew that claims being made by the city planner were based on cherry-picked data from a couple of reports put out by the National Association of Realtors and the American Planning Association. Instead of simply saying "NO!" to the city planner's proposal to implement new code restrictions on private property, she debunked each of his claims with alternative facts that supported different solutions. The new information revealed to City Council there were alternative solutions to the issues the planner was trying to address; they asked him to reconsider his proposal and present a new one at the next council meeting. Just saying "NO!" is not enough if you want to effect different outcomes.

Back at the start of this book, I talked about how the Citizen Ninja way would help you confidently deal with dominant government and political entities. Observing these eight Citizen Ninja rules will not only bolster your confidence to speak up, but they will guide your efforts to effect change in your community, engage in civil political discourse, activate your civic rights, and stand up to influential government agencies.

22

Nudging

Nudging is an innocuous psychological push to get you to agree with a desired viewpoint or engage in an action sought by the nudger. Nudging is a "gentler and kinder" coaxing that combines persuasion and suggestion. Unaware of being nudged, people feel they have a range of choices when they are actually being subtly pushed toward a desired outcome.

Expert marketers nudge the public all the time in television, radio, magazine, and website advertising. Movie scripts and documentaries also nudge to garner a desired response from the public. Well-crafted language and influential images may entice you to choose one product, service, or ideology over another.

Nudging isn't always this obvious.

So, it's not surprising that nudging is also used by politicians, corporations, and NPO/NGOs seeking to sway your opinion and decisions. Our job as Citizen Ninjas is to recognize, analyze, and question the nudge.

Surveys

Corporations or NPO/NGOs seeking public consensus often gather information on opinions about a particular issue through the use of surveys. You should expect these surveys to indirectly and subtly nudge public opinion. The language used is persuasive and carefully crafted to create a hierarchy of preferred choices; rarely will you see options for "other" or "no".

The online survey *Show Your Love San Diego* posted by the San Diego Foundation for example, offered citizens an opportunity to participate in the planning matrix to update the City of San Diego's urban development and transportation policies. According to their website, over 30,000 people participated in the survey. The data collected were used to shape San Diego's 50 to 100-year vision. The results of the survey are being used by local planning commissions and developers to support changes in traditional planning paradigms.

Recognize and Analyze

The San Diego Foundation, which promotes and funds a planning trend called "Smart Growth," offers an example of how NPO/NGOs may nudge people to support compact growth. Smart Growth calls for mixed-use, high-density urban development with easy access to transportation, services, and parks.

Show Your Love San Diego favors Smart Growth and seeks more focused input from the community at large to help planners and elected officials create a robust plan that people may want. Consider the following introduction to a section of the survey, wherein respondents will be asked to select one of four proposed scenarios for the region's future development.

The best we can do in predicting the future is build models of what the future might look like based on choices we can make today and then calculate, as best we can, what impact those visions of the future would have on things that matter most to us. Based on input from the public and experts in the region and at a national level, four different visions or "scenarios" of the future were designed. Importantly, all four scenarios accommodate future growth much more compactly than the region currently does, and all four include the same regional transportation improvements for both roads and public transportation. The scenarios differ most in the degree to which each provides the mix and kinds of housing people will want and will be able to afford in the future. The scenarios also differ in the degree of community and regional cooperation and organization needed to locate housing close to jobs, people close to public transportation, and the parks, stores, and places that people visit close to home.

The introduction reads nicely and the content is positive. But keep in mind when completing a survey who the authors are and what they are seeking before answering the survey questions or forming opinions. Instead of taking a survey at face value or accepting everything you read in a pamphlet, question what you see, hear, and read. For example, while watching a documentary on the effects of frack-ing, ask yourself who created the film and do they have a bias? Are they benefactors of oil production, or are they longtime supporters of the Sierra Club?

In this case, San Diego Foundation is the author and they encourage future compact development.

Read the passage again but this time through a Citizen Ninja lens. I have boldfaced words and phrases and attached a number that coordinates with my list of comments below. Put your opinions about Smart Growth aside and focus rather on how San Diego Foundation uses specific language to set the desired tone for this section of the survey.

The best we can do...

The word "best" is a superlative—good, better, best—and qualifies their effort. "We" automatically ties "us" to "them". The underlying message is that we are in this together and our thoughts, efforts, and choices are linked.

. . . in predicting the *future* is build models of what the *future* might look like based on choices we can make today and then calculate, as best we can, what impact those visions of the *future* would have on...

The word "future" is used several times for effect, and though it is prudent to plan for the future, they are looking to plan 50-100 years into the future. Ask yourself if planning that far ahead is possible given how quickly technology changes and improves.

. . . *things that matter most to us.*

The phrase "things that matter most to us" assumes we share the same priorities about what we care about. The word "most" is a superlative to indicate other options are not viable.

Based on input from *the public and experts in the region and at a national level...*

The word "public" is not specific. Do they mean civil society (NPO/NGOs) and/or experts? Telling us where the experts come from does not mean they are qualified.

. . . *four* different visions or "scenarios" of the *future* were designed.

The number of scenarios is fine but recognize there are no scenarios which offer a "no plan" or "no change" option. It would be like an insurance broker offering four insurance plans and saying that opting out is not an option.

Importantly, *all four scenarios accommodate future growth much more compactly than the region currently does, and all four include the same regional transportation improvements...*

These phrases tell you that all four scenarios include what future planning should incorporate—more compact growth and transportation improvements.

The scenarios differ most in the degree to which each provides the mix and kinds of housing **people will want . . .**

The phrase "people will want" assumes that the proposed scenarios are what people will want in the future and that San Diego Foundation's vision is the people's vision.

. . . and will be able to afford . . .

This is economic forecasting with no factual basis. **. . . in the future.** The scenarios also differ in the degree of community and **regional cooperation and organization needed to** locate housing close to jobs, people **close to public transportation**, and the **parks, stores, and places** that people visit **close to home.**

San Diego Foundation says that being close to jobs, close to parks, close to home is what matters most to us and that the only variance is how the region will need to cooperate and organize to achieve the vision.

Question

When you've recognized and analyzed, then question what you're seeing, reading, and hearing. If organizations are not honest about their predisposition, then it is up to us, as Citizen Ninjas, to draw attention to it. Had San Diego Foundation been deceptive they would not have written "Importantly, all four scenarios accommodate future growth much more compactly than the region currently does, and all four include the same regional transportation improvements for both roads and public transportation."

To address surveys that are not forthcoming write your objections in the margins or in the comment section box alerting the organization the survey is unfair or misleading. Then, work to expose the deceptive surveys: contact the originators of the survey to register a complaint, write editorials in the local newspaper, alert your social network, reach out to friendly journalists and radio talk show hosts, and ask other Citizen Ninjas to do the same. The more publicity you can garner, the more you expose the scheme.

When Nudging Becomes Bullying

Any person, agency, organization, movie producer, or advertiser is at liberty to nudge and coax the public. As Citizen Ninjas we need to be alert and question the nudge. Sometimes the nudge is so obviously biased that it is actually a bully tactic. In politics, respond critically when it is obvious that the intent is to elicit certain responses or changes in behavior toward desired ones. Persuasive language becomes bullying when it intimidates and coerces the public to make choices or form opinions that may not align with their own beliefs and values.

Topics like climate change, gun control, and abortion are extremely polarizing issues whose respective advocates are igniting a behavioral revolution. The people on each side of these issues are beyond nudging the public one way or the other; there's obvious intent to bully and influence. Resorting to intimidation and fallacies, individuals and groups are labeled "Climate Change Alarmists" or "Climate Change Deniers" and are barred from public deliberation. When nudging becomes bullying it's time for you to use your discretion and wield your four Citizen Ninja powers—civic knowledge, self-restraint, self-assertion, and self-reliance.

23

Visioning Meetings

itizen Ninjas' role in self-government is supported by the civic, electoral, and political opportunities, such as volunteering for a board position, voting, running for office, and delivering public comments. To enable and encourage robust community engagement, transparency laws define how different government agencies must provide public access to the management of the people's business. One of the mechanisms for transparent government is a "public visioning meeting".

Public visioning meetings, workshops, or forums—sometimes called charrettes—are organized by city staff at the behest of councils or boards to facilitate public deliberation on upcoming planning, zoning, or ordinance changes. For example, a workshop might be established to propose new codes or a change in zoning. Or the meeting may be to educate the council on new water or conservation restrictions. Other times public visioning

process might be initiated to get the public's consensus on the best way to update the general plan.

Be proactive. The earlier you engage, the more impact you have. Public visioning meetings often cover nudging. Use your four Citizen Ninja powers to determine when bully tactics are at play to neutralize attempts by the facilitator to bully, sway, or nudge the public's decision-making process.

Early Stages

Cities often hire a consulting firm to assist in scoping out a plan by providing expertise on a variety of technical elements. A parallel working group of early-stage decision makers—known as stakeholders—is formed to provide representation among government agencies, businesses, and NPO/NGOs. During the initial stages of the project the public is invited to participate in a visioning meeting in which the working group can share its progress and the public can give feedback and register an opinion.

Visioning Facilitators

Citizen Ninjas hope for robust and vibrant meetings led by a non-biased facilitator trained to listen to a variety of opinions, consider relevant facts, recognize competing positive values, and manage the discussion. Harmony is not the first word that comes to mind when I think about the public visioning process. Public issues almost always result in trade-offs, tough choices, and can lead to flaring emotions and discontent. Civil discourse can be achieved when citizen stakeholders know that final decisions are reached by consensus derived from reasoned public judgment and debate, rather than through manipulative tactics foisted on the public by the facilitator. Instead of seeking false consensus, the facilitator is asking the public for a consensus where everyone agrees that an idea or project is worthwhile and will compromise.

Bias

Citizen Ninjas are alert for facilitators, experts, and working groups who use manipulative tactics to nudge public opinion toward predetermined outcomes. The facilitator in these meetings is skilled in creating the *illusion* of public participation. When the manipulative tactics are skillfully employed, citizen stakeholders leave the meeting feeling they contributed to the decision making process when, in reality, the process was set up to produce a false consensus of opinion.

Facilitator Goals and Tactics

While attending a public forum or what I call the "Home Team Arena", ask yourself the following questions. If either answer is "yes" then employ the Citizen Ninja way to work with others to neutralize the facilitator.

1. Are the GOALS of the Home Team to nudge citizens toward a desired outcome and to defeat any opposition?

2. Is the Home Team deploying manipulative TACTICS such as setting the stage, creating the environment, controlling the message, manipulating the outcome, intimidating and ridiculing the opposition, or forcing consensus?

How Public Forums Work

All public forums are set up similarly. There is a podium, an expert panel table, an overhead projector and screen, an easel, chairs for the public, maps, documents, and food. Using a sports metaphor, the Visiting Team is made up of concerned citizens—the public. The Home Team, comprises facilitator/government agency/stakeholders who set the parameters.

When the intent is to manipulate the meeting toward a desired outcome, the Visiting Team tends to be underrepresented and uninformed like I was the first time I attended one. When the meeting begins, pay close attention to the process to determine if the Home Team is pressing for a predetermined outcome. Identifying the goals and tactics being used can reveal if bullying is being deployed. Home Teams who bully mean to polarize groups and disenfranchise individuals who deviate from the group; they mean to skew the meeting.

Bullying Strategy

Facilitators who skew public visioning meetings tend to follow a common script that Citizen Ninjas watch for. First, the City announces the public is invited to participate in the visioning meeting to help public officials make decisions on upcoming plans. To facilitate the meeting a team of experts is hired, the working group is present with a designated facilitator. Shills or accomplices who may not be from the community are invited to participate—unbeknownst to the public—to support the facilitator and sway public opinion.

Likable Facilitator

The facilitators are likeable, putting citizen participants at ease to elicit sympathy and agreement. The facilitator and shills are quick to identify dissenters and agitators in order to marginalize them as the bad guys using ad hominem attacks, for example, so that citizen stakeholders asking questions appear extreme, foolish, uneducated, or aggressive. All the while facilitators appear to be the friendly victim which subtly aligns naive citizen participants in favor of the desired outcome.

The public assumes that the facilitator's job is to play an impartial role directing the meeting, recording comments and feedback, and answering questions. In a skewed visioning meeting, the facilitator steers the public toward the desired outcome by the Home Team and the public servants who called the meeting.

Watch for Changes in Format

When the participants group is large with numerous identified agitators, the format of the meeting may change. Larger groups may be divided into smaller ones to achieve a divide and conquer effect. In smaller groups, the public is not able to hear everyone's comments and questions. Smaller groups seem more intimate, which subtly removes un-knowing citizens further from the process by herding small groups to different tables or into different rooms with a designated subordinate facilitator.

As the meeting proceeds discussion, comments, and responses to questions are "managed" to move the public to agree and support the desired outcome, while demeaning those posing contrary viewpoints. During the meeting, com-ments are recorded on flip pads, tabulated electronically, with sticky notes and so forth. I have witnessed helpers re-cording public comments deliberately change the intent of the comment to skew in favor of the proposed plan. Speak up and don't hesitate to correct such "tweeks" and request that it be rewritten into the record.

Identify Skewed Outcomes

The meeting ends when the facilitator feels the group has reached a consensus of opinion that supports the desired outcome. It is important the public's perception is that all opinions were considered so they leave feeling they partic-ipated in the process—even when they disagreed with the plan.

Anticipate multiple meetings when the public forum is for a general plan update, for example, or the plan covers a large region. All forums lead to a final presentation before the City Council or governing agency votes. At the general meeting, the team of experts present their findings to the public servants requesting the required public input. The experts (inaccurately) report they reached a consensus in support of the project. Having mitigated any political liabili-ty, the public servants vote their approval.

Be Aware

When the facilitator and cohorts are allowed to dominate the meeting and deploy manipulative tactics without any intervention by effective activists, the outcome of the meeting will be skewed toward their desired outcome. Citizen Ninjas neutralize these tactics to stimey reaching a (false) consensus. Nudging tactics only work when the participants are unaware they are being manipulated.

Being aware is central in effective activism. Discern the intensity of the manipulation and then use the Citizen Ninja way to respond.

The good news is that this manipulation can be neutralized. It does not take an army of activists to derail Home Team bullying. A few knowledgeable, organized Citizen Ninja activists can expose the facilitator's tactics. When this is accomplished, the covert purpose of the facilitator and public servants is derailed, giving Citizen Ninjas an opportunity to present alternative solutions and ideas without the facilitator and shills dominating the process and affronting them.

Unfortunately, public servants often proceed without the public's support. But at least they have been exposed and are politically liable. Gaining this leverage, you can employ the Citizen Ninja way to gain support to vote them out of office or initiate a recall election to boot them out. By neutralizing manipulative public visioning process, Citizen Ninjas reestablish citizen power and rights of self-determination.

Prepare for Nudging

When a public visioning meeting has been scheduled, it is best for Citizen Ninjas to prepare in case bully tactics are deployed. This motivates Citizen Ninjas to strategize. Unprepared citizen activists are likely to become anxious, defensive and angry when first subjected to bully tactics. Becoming victims, their emotional reactions make them vulnerable to shills. When citizens are struggling to be activists but are untrained in the Citizen Ninja way, they often overreact and fail to moderate their responses becoming bullies themselves. To stay on course, remember to question the Home Team's goals and tactics.

Neutralize the Facilitator

Coordinated manipulation within public visioning meetings can be neutralized. The following techniques to neutralizing a skewed public visioning meeting were adapted from Beverly Eakman's book, *How to Counter Group Manipulation Tactics: The Techniques of Unethical Consensus-Building Unmasked.*

Plan Ahead

To start, meet with a small group of Citizen Ninjas ahead of time in a different location to organize a seating plan, write out questions and talking points, select a videographer, and prepare for contingencies. Have a plan in case not every member of your group shows up or the meeting changed time and/or location. It is a good idea to designate someone to be in charge of chasing down the meeting details. If the meeting topic is controversial, the government agency may either schedule the meeting at an inconvenient time or make last-minute changes to the schedule or location.

Expect the forum to be a robust and vibrant meeting being led by a facilitator trained to listen to a variety of

opinions, who considers relevant facts, recognizes competing positive values, and manages the discussions to prevent
an escalation of underlying tensions. This is a best case
scenario! Notwithstanding, adopt the following plan in case
the facilitator intends to bully, sway, or nudge the public's
decision-making process.

Arrive Early

On the day of the event, arrive separately, like strangers.
Do not greet or make eye contact with each other. Arriv-
ing early provides an opportunity to identify possible shills.
One time, I overheard the facilitator actually give instruc-
tions to a shill on how to handle antagonists.

Depending on the size of your group, sit in a triangle,
diamond, or zigzag formation. Try not to sit together or
bunched in a cluster; appear scattered. If the participants
are divided into smaller groups at individual tables or in
rooms, make sure there is at least one member of your
group at each table or in each room. The reason to do this
is to appear numerous but separate. If you appear as one
group the facilitator can easily cull out multiple voices and
treat them as one voice.

Stick to the Plan

Stick to the
plan and
stay focused
throughout
the meeting.
When the meet-
ing is being recorded,
make sure the camera
is rolling. When the
facilitator is a bully
attempting to nudge

the public toward a desired outcome, a recording of these tactics is powerful evidence. This is the time for you to use Citizen Ninja skills and powers to neutralize the facilitator.

To establish your intent to be a team player, follow the rules established by the facilitator—at first. When you choose to be assertive, raise your hand for the microphone and read your carefully prepared question or comment in a professional voice.

Facilitators are trained to "reframe" your question or comment to "fit the narrative" to support their view. While the faciliator reframes what you said, wait patiently for him to finish, then point out the reframing missed your point. Repeat—verbatim—what you said originally. Organizers rarely hand over the microphone more than once, so hold on to it as long as you can. Continue to repeat your question or comment verbatim until it is addressed properly. Make sure to not change your tone of voice so it sounds emotional. Note the organizers will have a pad on an easel upon which to record your comment. Pay attention to what is written. If your question or comment is distorted, ask that it be corrected.

When the manipulation is confronted, facilitators squirm and show frustration. When the facilitator insists the meeting "move along," your Citizen Ninja cohorts can speak up to request the facilitator address your comment. One might say, for example: "You have not answered this lady's question. I would like to hear your answer please."

Maintain Composure

Maintain composure and a civil tone at all times. Shills will agitate and move to defend the facilitator. They will attempt to marginalize, intimidate, and insult you. Maintain your composure! When you have established you are the good guy and the facilitator and shills are the bad guys, release the microphone and wait for another Citizen Ninja to get the microphone to repeat the same tactic.

By staying calm and professional, Citizen Ninjas gain the sympathy of the audience and the facilitator will have lost control of the meeting. Often what happens is that by following these steps, you awaken unwitting participants who will join your team without even realizing their tacit participation.

Follow Through

Always wait until the meeting is adjourned before leaving. When you and your group have successfully neutralized the facilitator, the meeting will end without having reached a consensus and the facilitator will have failed in achieving the objective. When the adjournment is called, leave separately. Transparency laws stipulate that all comments are made public. Hold the government agency accountable to this by checking online that the comments were accurately recorded. Contact the agency and ask for a correction if there are discrepancies. Follow through after the meeting is as important as neutralizing a bully facilitator. The public needs to know there was no consensus.

It is lawful to record these meetings, which I support especially when polemic factions exist. Posting online, via YouTube™ for example, exposes the bully behavior, creates political pain for the public servants, and stimulates public engagement. Writing letters to the editor about the experience is also effective.

Focus on Truth and Justice

Keep in mind there are times when the government agency's agenda is so extensive and backed by powerful special interest groups, that all efforts fail and an opposed plan proceeds despite the opposition, which leads activists to become frustrated and even cynical. When this happens, I remind them that trying to control the outcome of our efforts is not the objective. Citizen Ninjas act on behalf of truth and justice and the conservancy of self-government. Strong strategic community engagement is needed, especially in the face of set-backs.

24

We Have Rights

America is exceptional because our government and its public servants are bound by the constraints set within the *Constitution* and the *Bill of Rights,* and their power is intended to be limited and checked by the executive, legislative, and judicial offices. This republican form of government supports the type of democracy where there is a presumption of equal representation, fairness, and justice, and where no single majority group has unilateral power.

The Constitution's purpose was not to establish a government of men but rather to institute a government of laws that protect our inalienable rights. In its first paragraph, the *Declaration of Independence* asserts we have inalienable birthrights that are protected under a rule of law that is in harmony with a higher divine law—the laws of Nature and Nature's God. These laws cannot be amended, taken away, or new ones be decreed by a monarch or issued by local petty dictators at their own discretion. The *Declaration of Independence* was a rejection of tyranny and a reclamation of individual sovereign power—self-government. Civil law builds on this foundation and creates order in our society. No person is supposed to be above the law, not even the president.

Citizen Stakeholders

State Constitutions also limit the reach of government, clarify its functions, and safeguard our rights. American citizens are endowed with intrinsic sovereign, independent and self-determining rights. Supported by our founding and state documents and laws, Citizen Ninjas work to preserve the power of self-government to keep it a representative republic that is of the people, by the people, and for the people. Citizen Ninjas actively engage in the public square, least we are sidelined by the government agencies and public private partnerships that increasingly dominate political and governmental landscapes.

A speaker at a conference I attended said, "If you are not at the table, you're what's for dinner" when describing the importance of being a business or NPO/NGO stakeholder working in partnership with government. His comment dramatically underscores the need for Citizen Ninjas to understand their rights.

First Amendment

The rights of citizens to engage in the political process are found in the *Bill of Rights,* which is the first of the ten amendments to the Constitution.

Congress shall make no law respecting an establishment of religion, or prohibiting the free exercise thereof; or abridging the freedom of speech, or of the press; or the right of the people peaceably to assemble, and to petition the Government for a redress of grievances.   —Amendment 1

The right to communicate with or about the government is protected in the First Amendment. Congress is forbidden to pass laws that prevent us from publicly expressing our opinions. The First Amendment is comprised of five rights.

Rights Protected by the 1st Amendment

1) Freedom of speech—the government cannot censor or limit speech; this includes 'symbolic speech' as in wearing clothing, jewelry, or buttons in protest. Some speech can be limited as in the case of 'hate' speech or 'clear and present danger' speech like yelling "Fire!" when there isn't one.

2) Freedom of the press—the media have the right to print and distribute information.

3) Right to peaceful assembly—the public may come together in the form of a protest or association regardless of the message. Public order is taken into consideration and may at times restrict the people's right to assemble.

4) Right to petition the government for redress of grievances—the public has the right to expose government misconduct and lawlessness and may file complaints in order to resolve issues.

5) Freedom of religion—the government is prohibited from establishing an official religion. Citizens are free to select the religion of their choice.

Anthony M. Kennedy, Associate Justice of the US Supreme Court, said: "The right to think is the beginning of freedom, and speech must be protected from the government because speech is the beginning of thought." *The Declaration of Independence,* the *Constitution of the United States,* and its *Bill of Rights* are standard bearers for freedom and justice.

Transparency Laws

Transparency laws, also known as sunshine laws, require that certain actions by government agencies be open and available to the public. Transparency laws favor the people's right of access and placing the burden on government to prove it has the authority to obstruct our access.

In this section I am using California's transparency laws as an example, but it is important to read the laws in your state of residence because they vary between states. The *Freedom of Information Act* (FOIA) is a federal transparency law that follows similar guidelines and statutes as the states'.

Request for Public Records

The *California Public Records Act* and the *California Open Meeting Act,* for example, guarantee that we have access to public records and legislate how public meetings are presided over. Under the terms of these laws, any person or the media can request records for various reasons from government agencies. It might be to investigate an official's correspondence, financial reports, or datebook, for example. The only fees allowed are for photocopying, not for search and retrieval time.

While document requests generally do not require a statement of purpose, they should be written and specific, stating the identity of persons or agencies, dates, and the format in which you wish to receive the information. Always keep a copy.

Government employees search only for what is requested, which is why being very specific is important. They are not required to interpret ambiguity in the request. The agency must acknowledge receiving the request within ten days. The agency may deny a records request based on the statutes; which the person making the request can appeal.

Government Transparency

The California *Brown Act* legislates how public meetings can be conducted. Public agencies exist to conduct business for the public and the public has a right to know what, why, and how decisions are being made. The need for government confidentiality must be balanced against the importance of public access.

The public has the right to be notified of agenda items, to have access to documents distributed to the members of the council, to be free from discrimination, to record the meeting, and to speak without identifying oneself. Additionally transparency laws define what constitutes "a meeting", agenda requirements, public's rights, what may be done in closed sessions—such as contract negotiations, staff evaluations, disciplinary action—and the consequences for violation.

Consider Antonio who had a blighted house on his street where vagrants and druggies were squatting, without power or water. The City had done nothing, despite Antonio's complaints to City staff, the police, and the health department. Marcus, his co-worker, advised Antonio to use the City Council meeting to get action! Marcus, a seasoned Citizen Ninja, explained that because the Council is elected to represent the town's citizen, they are required to listen if he expresses his concerns at the "Public Microphone". He offered to accompany him.

Marcus and Antonio arrived early to the Council meeting to have time to fill out speaker's slips. When the Clerk called

Antonio's name, he delivered a three minute public comment to the Council. Marco followed up with another three minute comment about the blighted house. The next day, they separately followed up with an email to each Council member, which ensured the complaint was entered into the public record.

> Governance by Public Private Partnerships has a kind of alluring glitter that hides its faults.

Marcus supported Antonio in his efforts to get the City to "do something" about the blighted house and the vagrants, while teaching him how to be an "activist"—a Citizen Ninja. Empowered, Antonio gathered several neighbors to attend the next City Council meeting to speak. Soon after the second public mic blast, the City cleared out the squatters, redirected them to a local charity, and "red-tagged" the blighted house.

Boards & Commissions Transparency

Fortunately, laws like the California *Bagley-Keene Open Meeting Act* extend the same transparency requirements to State boards and commissions members, who are usually appointed. To expect boards and commissions conduct business openly is especially important because it is within these organizations that public private partnerships are often formed. The influential stakeholders—government, business, and NPO/NGOs— often make decisions before bringing them to the public for comment, which undermines transparency.

The *Bagley-Keene Act,* for example, requires that a seat be reserved at the table for the public during the decision-making process. Often board members would rather conduct the people's business more efficiently and avoid involving the public in consensus building. Other times they sidestep the frustrating process of public deliberation with a quick public comment period scheduled at inconvenient times, which get changed at the last minute, leading to poor attendance and a lack of participation by the public.

To counter the tendency of Boards to thwart public participation, Citizen Ninjas prepare for contingencies, such as contacting the organizers the day before a meeting to confirm it's time and place.

Successful grassroots activism uses the Citizen Ninja way and the four Citizen Ninja powers in conjunction with understanding your rights and knowing the law is on the people's side. Take the time to learn and understand the laws in your state so you can act with boldness and confidence.

25

We Are the Power!

To better understand why it's important for Citizen Ninjas to be active citizen stakeholders, we need to take a look at how partnerships between government agencies, and favored corporations and selected NPO/NGOs impact our right to participate in government. Dominant public private partnerships that do not include citizen stakeholders represent a shift in power from self-government to governance by stakeholders. Stakeholders are individuals or groups who have an interest in public policy. By wielding their civic powers, Citizen Ninjas reclaim their rightful place at the stakeholder table. We, the citizen stakeholders, are the true power; all we have to do is exercise it.

Let's start by learning the concept behind public private partnership (PPPs). "We can no longer operate in silos" is a phrase often used by change agents, like planners, businesses, NPO/NGOs, economists, and others to illustrate and explain why, as a society, we must break down our automatic inclination to conduct 'business as usual,' and why our system of self-government should be expanded to include PPPs. Change agents influence civil society, industry, and government. They have a vision for how future organizational structures, cultural values, and people's perspectives can transform to something greater. Some famous change agents include: Dr. Martin Luther King, the catalyst for the civil rights movement; Steve Jobs' iPhone; the creators of the Internet, who revolutionized communications, business, and commerce; and feminist Susan B. Anthony, who championed the suffrage movement and women's right to vote. PPPs are the new model for an integrated system of government—governance by stakeholders.

Breaking Down Silos

The word silos—stand-alone containers that store agricultural bulk material—is today's metaphor to describe how our society is organized. In politics, silos are called sectors: the government sector, the business sector, the civil society (NPO/NGO) sector, and the public (citizen) sector. Sectors are distinct, independent silos that operate within their own established systems; each one sees itself as separate from the others and seeks to protect its interests.

Catalysts who are pushing for a change in governance criticize silo constructs that inevitably isolate stakeholders instead of integrating them. They claim that independent silos do not communicate or cooperate well with each other, resulting in an overall, inefficient system that often leads to competing or incompatible goals; sometimes with unintended consequences.

SILO STAKEHOLDERS

This happens frequently with changes in zoning. For example, in a coastal city, the City Council made the decision to expand industrial zoning in order to increase merchant ship activity. People living in the surrounding community were furious when they heard about the decision. Conflicts and legal battles ensued. The theory is that if City Council had worked to integrate all the stakeholder silos—marine merchants, citizens, city council, and housing advocacy NPO/NGOs—from the start, financial resources, time, and energy would have been saved rather than spent.

Technology Helps Remove Silos

Businesses are built around people who occupy and work in different departments, such as a sales department, a human resources department, an accounting department, and so on. Each department has a particular way of operating. When a job is approved, the account is processed within each department according to its function. Now think about "cloud technology", which enables people to work in non-linear ways across departmental boundaries. They interface and network, creating more efficiency. Cloud technology facilitates the breakdown of departmental 'silos' in the workplace.

Similarly impactful is the use of technology to facilitate the practice of "crowdfunding". Crowdfunding is a fundraising mechanism that breaks down small donor 'silos'. It allows fundraising initiators, like film producers, research scientists, or civic leaders, to reach out via the Internet to a larger number of people than exist in their own sphere of influence, to fund a project or venture. Crowdfunding correspondingly allows smaller donors to pool their mon-

DECLARATION of INDEPENDENCE

...We mutually pledge to each other our Lives, our Fortunes, and our Sacred Honor.

THOMAS JEFFERSON
Draftsman of US Declaration of Independence,
3rd US President

ey toward a project or venture so they can have more impact together as one source of funding.

Using technology such as the Internet or the cloud to facilitate cooperation and efficiency is described by its proponents as "progress." Those promoting stakeholder governance seek the same goals. They believe we build cooperation and increase efficiency by integrating the government, business, NPO/NGOs, and citizen silos. What is evolving is a new type of participatory democracy.

Beyond The Allure

Looking past the sparkle of this new participatory democracy, we see it is governance by non-elected, appointed regional associations and commissions, and regulatory agencies partnering with favored businesses and selected NPO/NGO stakeholders. Instead of integrating all the stakeholders—business, regional boards, NPO/NGO, and citizen—there is a consolidation of powers that often excludes the citizen. Increasingly, PPPs subordinate local, city and county decisions as they have in regional master plans.

Regional projects like Southern Florida's *SEVEN/50 Plan* (7 counties/50 years) and Northern California's nine-county *Plan Bay Area 2040* for example, bring together regional Metropolitan Planning Organizations (MPOs), transportation agencies, environmental NGOs, and foundations with corporate partners, to push through paradigm shifts in planning—focus on smart growth versus suburban development that cover large regions. After these entities have spent considerable time, money, and resources to come up with a regional plan, they invite the public to workshops to present their proposed plans and get feedback.

Despite public outreach for the California *Plan Bay Area,* for example, it is estimated that less than one percent of the seven million inhabitants were reached for public comment. This really isn't a surprising statistic when you consider that these regional plans do not originate in local towns and small cities. Only citizens and civil society organizations who are paying attention and are informed show up. Without proper representation and despite a relatively small band of citizens who opposed the plan, *Plan Bay Area* was adopted by each of the governing agencies, leaving local jurisdictions within the nine counties to struggle with compliance.

Citizens Can Make a Difference

The theory is that multilevel stakeholder governance—integrated silos—creates more efficiency and greater regional cooperation. In this silo scenario MPOs are tasked with overseeing and managing other areas which previously were handled at the local level. Massachusetts' *Sustainable Communities Act* (H1859), California's *Sustainable Communities Strategies Planning Act* (SB 375), and *Smart, Green, & Growing,* the tag line for Maryland's *Sustainable Communities Act* (AB475) are three examples that mandate regional MPOs to coordinate land use,

transportation, affordable housing, and air quality. Placing this type of legislation in the hands of regional associations effectively removes local decision making authority and undermines the power of self-government.

Citizen stakeholders lose influence and their power is eroded when they are not informed and do not participate in government affairs. Citizen Ninjas, on the other hand pay attention, so when a regional plan is in the works, we are there right from the beginning, insisting on our right to be part of the deliberative process. Citizen Ninjas in south Florida are doing just that. Their work has culminated in three counties opting out of the seven county plan.

Be a Citizen Stakeholder

Participatory democracy by definition should include the citizen stakeholder. We, the people, are entitled by law to be involved—to have a voice. Instead we get squeezed out by the more influential and better informed "insider" stakeholders. When citizens finally do get to participate at a public workshop, they sense facilitators are seeking false consensus to approve the plans rather than asking for their ideas and opinions. PPPs that do not equally include citizen stakeholders are in conflict with the American values of self-government.

Consider who Citizen Ninja Jay found out the County Board of Supervisors was considering zoning changes near a local wetlands preserve to accommodate a new residential mixed use facility. Without hesitation, he called his District Representative to relay his concerns about the preserve and related potential environmental impacts. The District Rep told him not to worry, that the staff under the Board's direction had pulled together a variety of economic and land use experts—stakeholders—to study impacts and opportunities, as well as work with the project developer, contractor, and architect.

When Jay asked to be a part of the committee as a citizen representative, the District Rep dismissed him. "It's not necessary. Our staff will manage." After pressing his concerns with all five County Board Commissioners, Jay was finally invited to be part of the committee as a citizen stakeholder. Participatory democracy is a redundant system of government when we have Citizen Ninjas who are committed to civic engagement. To stand up to dominant power, Jay used all of his Citizen Ninja powers. He knew the rules, he was professional, he didn't take no for an answer, and he took the lead instead of waiting for someone else to address the situation.

Claim Your Power

Naturally evolving change at the grassroots level is preferable to top-down regional autocratic dictates. When powerful stakeholders impose an agenda on you, it can trigger flaring emotions, anger, confusion, chaos, and distrust. The answer to this shift from self-government to governance by stakeholders is for you to claim your seat at the stakeholder table. As a Citizen Ninja you achieve this by participating and interacting in the public square, and by adapting how you engage so you can effectively stand up and claim your power.

26

Citizen Ninja Role Model

O ur earliest American civic role models are our forefathers, our revolutionary ancestors, and the framers of our United States Constitution. Through courageous perseverance and self-sacrifice, they provided future generations with a sustainable framework, which supports a just government that is of the people, by the people, and for the people. Civil society and self-government can be maintained if we work diligently toward this end. Citizen Ninjas who make a commitment to be actively engaged are important role models of civic responsibility.

Role models are important to society because they provide us with examples of how we might behave, they set a bar for achievement, and they inspire us to envision how their success could be our own. Role models tend to have several characteristics in common: they have a clear set of values, they lead by example, they are passionate about a cause or belief, they are resilient and perseverant, and they like working with others. Citizen Ninja role models also share these same characteristics. Let's take a look.

Clear Set of Values

The primary values that support your Citizen Ninja activism are captured in the four Citizen Ninja powers.

1. Civic Knowledge:

As a Citizen Ninja, you know pertinent

rules and laws, and understand your civic rights within that framework. This allows you to safely yet boldly navigate the public square.

2. Self-Restraint:

Self-restraint means you have the patience and discipline to discern environments, situations, and issues before engaging. This allows you to have measured and strategic responses rather than emotional gut reactions.

3. Self-Assertion:

Self-assertion is the willingness to step out of your comfort zone and engage in the public square. You can do this confidently because you are willing to practice and apply the Citizen Ninja way; the tactics and tools that allow you to be effective and successful. Your fear recedes as your confidence grows.

4. Self-Reliance:

As a Citizen Ninja, you believe that self-government is preserved when individuals like yourself participate in civic affairs, engage in civil political discourse, and work with other members of the community as citizen stakeholders.

Lead By Example

As a Citizen Ninja role model you are a special breed because you're not only unafraid to talk the talk—you also walk the walk. In other words, when you see or read about injustice, deviation from proper political ethics, or outright corruption, you engage. Instead of channeling outrage through effective civic activism, most people stay home, complain, or bully others who disagree with them. They never seem to be sufficiently motivated to effect any productive change. As you learned, there are a range of ways to engage, and each varies in intensity. Regardless of where you are on your activism journey, recognize that when you engage effectively, you also lead by example. You can inspire others.

Passion

Activists by definition are driven by strong beliefs and convictions. These characteristics are what move them to action. As a Citizen Ninja role model, your dedication to justice, freedom, and truth inspires others. Ordinary citizens who witness Citizen Ninjas in action will be so inspired by your confidence, knowledge, and self-restraint that they will often inquire how you can remain so calm in the face of disagreeable people and bullies. When you inspire people with your passion you become a Citizen Ninja role model. But you now know that passion is not enough and therefore strive to channel your passion into effective strategic action. You are faithful to the Citizen Ninja way.

Resilience and Perseverance

As a Citizen Ninja you are determined and committed. Not only do you demonstrate initiative and drive, you are undeterred by environmental factors that get in the way of your activity. You are resilient in the face of adversity because you know how to face the public successfully. It is easier to persevere when your efforts are rewarded with productive change. But even when your efforts are thwarted you find solace knowing you attempted some measure of civil intervention in the face of corruption, deviance, or injustice. The Citizen Ninja way is so effective that your activism actually becomes gratifying and stimulating. The more you participate in government and civil political discourse, the more your actions seamlessly develop into daily habits.

Working with Others

As a Citizen Ninja, you are trained to rely on yourself first and then reach out toward the needs of your community.

When you manage to obtain this powerful balance between passionate individual activism and community involvement you can effectively stand up to entrenched power. Remain mindful that citizen stakeholders who demand their rightful seat at the table will ensure an enduring representative republic. Furthermore, when members of the community witness your productive civic participation, it may inspire them to become Citizen Ninjas as well.

Our Pledge is Our Promise

The Pledge of Allegiance is your promise to hold the republic to its standard—liberty and justice for all. When you recite the pledge you make a promise to engage and exercise your civic rights. Elected officials take an oath; American citizens make a promise.

I Pledge Allegiance To the Flag Of the United States of America And to the Republic For Which It Stands; One Nation under God, Indivisible, With Liberty And Justice For All.

Every word in the pledge is important and warrants your attention. For Citizen Ninjas the first word, "I", is probably the most important, because no action will take place unless it is preceded by an "individual" making the choice to act—or to pledge in this case. The word "United" means that we are cohesive and integrated, and the word "Republic" underscores we are a recognized sovereign state that is of the people, by the people, and for the people. "Under God", added in the 1950s, sets an ethical and moral standard on which civil society depends. "Indivisible" means our nation is not only united, it is incapable of being divided. The word "Liberty" reminds us we have inalienable rights and are free to live our own lives without fear of retaliation. Finishing the pledge with the words "Justice for All" highlights the idea that "no one" is above the law. We are a nation with rules of law that apply to everyone equally.

When you say the pledge, you are saying you are steadfast in your commitment to stand up in the public square to defend inalienable rights, seek justice, and counter public servants who would undermine their oath of office to "support and defend the Constitution of the United States against all enemies, foreign and domestic."

Final Thoughts

We are all bound to each other by the simple but extraordinary good fortune that we are American citizens. Each day the news delivers heart-wrenching examples of people around the world willing to sacrifice everything they have in an effort to achieve the freedoms we enjoy as Americans. The United States is exceptional not just because of her economic standing, her military strength, or her ingenuity. She is exceptional because she is the sum total of her parts—the people. Imagine what it could mean if we all took our civic responsibility to heart.

Pericles, the ancient Greek statesman and orator, said, "Just because you do not take an interest in politics does

not mean politics will not take an interest in you." The political system continues whether we partici-
pate or not. Unfortunately, our citizenry's
silence and dis-engagement are under-
standably interpreted by public
servants as tacit agreements with
the decisions being made. This is
unacceptable and conflicts with
our political system's intended
goals of self-determination.

I encourage you to join me and other
activists to make the choice for liberty,
to follow the Citizen Ninja way, and to
exercise your Citizen Ninja powers of civic
knowledge, self-restraint, self-assertion, and
self-reliance. Your noble actions *today*
will sustain and inspire future generations *tomorrow.*

Arne Ratermanis is a creative director, graphic designer and illustrator residing in San Diego, California. Arne has been drawing and illustrating his whole life. Over the past 25 years, his strong sense of design has heavily influenced his vector-based illustration work.

Besides advertising and marketing, Arne's illustrations have appeared in various science fiction, fantasy and pop culture themed publications including *Fantastyka, Farscape Magazine, TV Guide* and *Wizard Magazine*. In addition, his depictions of comic book superheroes have been selected for inclusion into San Diego Comic-Con International's annual souvenir book for over 10 years and counting. Arne's work has been recognized by local, regional, and national illustration and design awards, as well as client industry honors.

Website: www.ratermanis.daportfolio.com

Mary Baker is a political activist, author, and educator residing in Poway, California. She leads several non-profit organizations, has received volunteerism awards for community service, and serves on different committees in the City of Poway.

Citizen Ninja: Stand Up to Power! was inspired by an activism workshop Mary created called *How to Become a Citizen Ninja,* a training on how to participate in the civic process, engage in civil political discourse, and neutralize bullies. Mary has trained over 800 citizens on the art of effective and sustaining activism.

Mary holds a Bachelor of Arts from Middlebury College where she graduated Cum Laude. She grew up in Europe. In her spare time, Mary enjoys tutoring high school students in French and Spanish, which she speaks fluently. Mary has been married for 27 years and has two children.

Website: www.themarybaker.com

Citizen Ninja™

How to Become a Citizen Ninja™

The framers of our Constitution knew that to preserve our blessings of liberty, the Republic would require self-governing citizens.

- Do you worry about being marginalized if you express your opinion in public?

- Have you been bullied in a public forum or town hall meeting?

- Do you wonder if civil discourse is even possble?

How to Become a Citizen Ninja™ is a workshop designed for Americans who recognize they have a duty to engage in the civic process but are unsure how to go about it or are fearful of bully tactics being used against them.

"Learn how to sideline your fears! This workshop will teach you how to exercise your civic responsibility in the public arena effectively and with confidence." —Mary Baker

Host a Workshop or Key Note

If your organization wants to activate its members, this is the workshop for you. Contact us by emailing marybaker@citizenninja.org to schedule a workshop or talk in your area.

- *How to Become a Citizen Ninja™* — full day workshop.

- *Citizen Ninja™ Fast Track* — three-hour seminar.

- Citizen Ninja™ Lunch & Learn — one-hour Key Note.

email: marybaker@citizenninja.org

Printed in the USA
CPSIA information can be obtained
at www.ICGtesting.com
JSHW022339140824
68134JS00019B/1570

9 781579 512200